Free Will and Determinism in Criminology and Criminal Justice

Law, Crime and Law Enforcement

Anthony Walsh, PhD
Boise State University, Idaho, USA

Free Will and Determinism in Criminology and Criminal Justice

nova science publishers
New York

Library of Congress Cataloging-in-Publication Data

ISBN: 979-8-88697-621-2

Published by Nova Science Publishers, Inc. † New York

Table of Contents

Preface

Few concepts bedevil the social sciences as much as the problem of free will (or free mind). It is particularly problematic for criminology and criminal justice because these are disciplines that involve the very character of the people they deal with and how we should treat them. There is a liberal-conservative divide on the issue which reveals itself in the theories they favor as the best explanations for serious criminal behavior. Liberals tend to hold an external locus of control and are skeptical about the idea of free will, and conservatives tend to favor an internal locus of control and believe in free will. Liberals thus tend to favor explanations for criminal behavior that are external to criminals such as an unfair economic system or criminal justice bias, which tends to excuse criminals, whereas conservatives tend to favor internal explanations such as low self-control or a lack of empathy, which does not. In terms of responding to criminal behavior, there have been calls to abandon the idea of punishment and abolish prisons. Liberals tend to view such recommendations as humanitarian and conservatives tend to view them as incredibly naïve. The greater tendency of liberals to hold an external locus of control and their skepticism about free will leads them to view people's behavior as largely beyond their control, which accounts for their punishment abolitionist stance. Conservatives tend to have an internal locus of control and hold free will beliefs, which leads to a more punitive stance toward criminals. We hold people morally responsible for what they do only if we believe that they have the ability to make reasoned choices to act or not to act morally.

Free will is often juxtaposed to determinism, and although I argue that free will beliefs are important for upholding the humanity and dignity of people, I do not disavow determinism as believers in libertarian free will do. Libertarians view free will as the ability to choose a course of action independent of any external influence or internal natural inclination. This implicitly assumes human freedom from all externalities, but we cannot detach ourselves from externalities and remain functioning human beings. Our self-identities and patterns of reasoning and desiring are continually constituted and modified by their ongoing engagement with other people, our culture, and our world. It is hard determinism that I disavow. Hard determinism is all about externalities and the volitional actor is completely removed from consideration.

Belief in free will does not require that determinism be false, only that hard determinism as it relates to human actions be false. Science demonstrates conclusively that determinism is true, but this only rules out volitional behavior if one views free will and determinism as mutually exclusive. Compatibilism is the view that free will and "soft" determinism are compatible and is the position on the issue held by most modern philosophers. In regard to criminal behavior, compatibilism says that criminals choose to act criminally (the free will component) but their personality traits and the circumstance of their lives make their choices understandable (the determinism component).

I have written many books and research articles on the genetics and neurobiological factors associated with criminal behavior, but have maintained a belief in compatibilist free will. These genetic and neurobiological factors, in concert with environmental factors, *influence* (sometimes strongly, sometimes weakly) but do not constitute necessary and sufficient determinants of the behavior in question. To believe that criminals have absolutely no choice other than to engage in crime is to reduce them to irrational automatons. I look at the challenges to free will supposedly made by genetics and the neurosciences and find them less muscular than many propose, although they are fascinating to engage with. I also look at the criminogenic influence of non-belief in free will and in holding an external locus on control, look at the classical and positivist schools of thought, and conclude with a chapter on why we punish from an evolutionary standpoint.

Chapter One

The Issue of Free Will and Determinism

An Age-Old Question

Almost 50 years ago, Schafer (1976) wrote: "The problem of man's free will is critically important to criminological views, despite its almost insoluble nature and the inordinate Sisyphean intellectual labor required even to take sides in the centuries-old dispute" (p. 481).

The issue of free will has indeed bedeviled philosophers for centuries, even though the labor required to engage it is a lot more fun than endlessly rolling boulders up mountains. Since the great minds across the ages have not come to a consensus on this matter, we can hardly claim to resolve it here. Nevertheless, Schafer is correct; the issue of free will versus determinism is central to many issues in criminology and criminal justice. Wanting to be considered scientists, most criminologists deem it imperative that they eschew metaphysical constructs such as free will and plant their banners securely in deterministic cause and effect. Others deride this as "physics envy," and claim that positivism, which they view as a "boo word," is inappropriate for understanding human action. As for criminal justice; the issue intrudes heavily on researchers' beliefs about criminal responsibility, rehabilitative efforts, and punishment.

The polarization of the free will/determinism issue was exemplified in the 20th century by the behaviorist psychologist B. F. Skinner, who insisted that we don't have free will but keep pretending that we do, and the existentialist philosopher J. P. Sartre who insisted that we have free will but keep pretending that we don't. The positions on the issue of these two men are extreme versions that brook no compromise and thus we are confronted with a Manichean choice on the issue; either we are completely determined or, as Sartre insisted, we are "condemned to be free." That is, we are free to make our own choices but we are also condemned to bear the responsibility for the consequences of those choices.

Historically, much of the Western philosophical work on the free will/determinism issue has been written within a theological framework (Roskies, 2006). Christian philosophers maintain that we have been endowed by God with the ability to make free choices, and those choices should be faithful to God's commands, although we are granted the freedom to decide that they won't be. The choice to accept or reject God must be free and not coerced if the choice is to be sincere. Atheist philosophers contend that free will is as illusionary as God and that our thoughts and actions are fully determined by our genes and our past experiences encoded in the wiring of our brains. They may also argue that if God exists and is omniscient, He knows everything that will be in the future, including everyone's behavior. This entails for them (since God cannot be wrong) that everything you or I do is predestined, and thus we cannot have free will. Of course, Christian philosophers have responded to this objection, but suffice to say that the issue was a hugely important one because it involved praise and blame in this world and ultimately reward and punishment in the next. The same concepts of praise and blame and reward and punishment are central to our discipline. A good God would not punish sinners if their behavior is fully determined, so how accountable should we hold criminals for their behavior?

Defining Free Will and Determinism

Let us first define free will and determinism succinctly in their most extreme forms. Libertarian free will is defined as the ability to choose a course of action independent of, or even in defiance of, any external or internal influences. This kind of free will implicitly assumes freedom from all externalities, but our subjective sense of self and our patterns of reasoning and desiring are never wholly our own. They are not entirely self-generated phenomena, nor can they be for we cannot detach ourselves from all externalities and remain functioning human beings. Rather, our self-identities and patterns of reasoning and desiring are continually constituted and modified by their ongoing engagement with other people, our culture, and our world. John Donne's 17th-century sermon containing the well-known line "No man is an island" emphasizes how human beings are inextricably connected to each other, and how important the connection is for our well-being and survival.

Hard determinism is all about externalities and is defined by the notion that one's choice of action in any situation is the necessary result of a sequence of outside causes channeled through one's genetic makeup, developmental experiences, and the current situation and that one cannot do other than what one does. The volitional actor is completely removed from consideration in this view. Of course, there are positions between these two extremes such as "soft" determinism, which allows for limited free will, and compatibilism, which maintains that free will and determinism are not incompatible and that we need both concepts to understand human beings and their actions.

When we speak of determinism, we mean that every event stands in some causal relationship to antecedent events. Determinism is a position relating to how the world is said to operate and is a position held by all scientists; what would it be for a scientist *not* to be a determinist? However, I am sure that no social scientist would claim that it is the case that given X, Y *will* occur when discussing human action. Rather, the claim is that given X, Y has some *probability* of occurring. We are all determinists in this sense, but when investigating human behavior our most inclusive models do not come near to explaining even one-half of the variance in criminality. This is true even in the models that include a slew of genetic, personality, and demographic predictor variables. We may blame this on poorly specified models and/or inadequate measuring instruments, but I am inclined to opt for locating much of the "missing" variance in human agency (self-efficacy). To have a sense of agency in any meaningful way, we must believe that we are the masters of our own fate regardless of the "truth" of that conviction, because if we believe it is true it is true in its consequences.

Although I have said that no social scientist would claim that it is the case that given X, Y *will* occur, many subconsciously view determinism through the same lens as determinism in sciences such as classical physics and chemistry. Al-Hoorie discusses fundamental differences between the hard sciences and the social sciences and states that the

> uniqueness of the social sciences might lie in people's ability to choose how to behave. Particles and molecules do not make choices, as their behaviour is predetermined and

> predictable by physical and chemical laws. That such precise predictability is absent in human behaviour is a strong argument for our ability to exercise free will through rational thought. In fact, it is the human ability to think and make rational choices that underlies ethical and moral judgments, for example deeming humans worthy of praise and reward for good behaviour, and answerable for wrongdoing. (2014, p. 55)

One of the sticking points in this issue is the position of hard determinists who aver that free will requires that determinism be false. Science demonstrates conclusively that determinism is true; therefore, they say, science proves we do not have free will. The problem with this syllogism is that its major premise is untrue; the free will argument does not require that determinism be false. I believe that Karl Marx got it right when he asserted that humans make their own history, but they make it from cloth they did not weave themselves. Left realist Steven Box (1987, p. 29) put this in a criminological context when he asserted that people *choose* to act criminally, and "their choice makes them responsible, but the conditions make the choice comprehensible." Contrary to Box's position, one often gets the impression that many criminologists want to go beyond comprehensibility to blame everything and anybody for crime except those who commit it. In their view, criminals are no freer to choose their life's direction than dead leaves blown hither and thither the vagaries of the November winds can choose which way to drift.

Neither should we go to the opposite extreme and confuse free will with unpredictability, as Greek philosopher Epicurus did by deducing free will from Democritus' atomic theory within which the swerve of an atom can occur without cause (Huby, 1967). Roman philosopher Lucretius developed a theory of free will based on that idea: "The atoms do not move in straight or uniform lines; there is in their motion an incalculable declination or deviation, an elemental spontaneity that runs through all things and culminates in man's free will" (in Durant, 1944, pp. 150–151). The modern version of this is based on Heisenberg's quantum mechanical principle of uncertainty, which has been used to affirm a libertarian free will (Schuster, 2009). Quantum phenomena are random, but they are statistically predictable. We cannot control random events and thus we cannot freely influence them, but would you want the kind of freedom that renders it impossible to probabilistically predict your behavior? The firing of neurons without reference to what is actually occurring in the world outside one's addled brain is one of the defining features of unmedicated schizophrenia, and I assume that being in that sad condition is not anyone's idea of freedom. As sociologist Max Weber said, this kind of "freedom" is "the privilege of the insane" (in Eliaeson, 2002, p. 35).

If free will is taken to mean action without a cause, all actions would be unpredictable and chaos would reign. The notion of unpredictability prior to observation may be characteristic of quantum mechanics, but in human affairs, it would be disastrous. Everything in the universe has a cause (even quantum phenomena, despite their weirdness); we belong to that universe, so what we think and do have causes. Agreeing to this does not commit us to hard determinism, since we are capable of causing our own creative thoughts and actions. If we are not responsible for our own behavior, then praise and blame alike are pointless. Why give medals to brave soldiers or praise and admiration to creative scientists, writers, and artists, and why blame and punish criminals for their bad actions if they could not have done otherwise? Certainly, what people do, good or bad, has a long causal chain traceable (in principle) to a complex mixture of their genomes, their brains, and their developmental experiences, but these are the cards dealt to us and we must play them the best we can. Some of us get royal flushes; others do no better than a pair of twos, but it is the choices we make given the hands we are dealt that are praiseworthy or blameworthy.

It might well be that soft determinism is necessary for free will, because if I did not think that what I do produces meaningful consequences, why would I do anything? All rational action, coaching, training, tutelage, and guidance are softly deterministic in the sense that they are designed to produce (cause) desired effects. We debate, educate, counsel, and write books under the assumption that we can change the minds of others, whom we assume are free to accept or reject what we propose. I know that I am a free agent and that living according to that position is necessary for self-efficacy, but I also know that my agency is constrained or enabled by my temperament, upbringing, knowledge, conscience, physical and cognitive abilities and disabilities, the size of my bank account, and the constraints imposed on me by others. But without a belief in free will or agency—our ability to shape our own worlds—our minds would be imprisoned in the deadly *Que sera, sera* fatalism that Walter Miller (1958) found infecting crime-ridden lower-class neighborhoods in his focal concerns theory.

Some believe that any kind of talk about our behavior that evokes external causes detracts from our freedom and dignity, which is counterintuitive. People who know us make conscious and subconscious predictions about us every day based on their knowledge of us. Let us say that I know Joe has found a wallet containing a considerable sum of money and I predict that he will turn it over to the police with the contents intact. By making that prediction, have I turned Joe into an automaton not free to do otherwise? I have made a prediction based on my understanding of Joe's moral character, thus Joe's moral character "determined" his moral choice. You may call Joe's behavior determined if you like because, after all, I did predict his behavior. Or you can call it free will just as well, since it was *his* moral character that led to his decision. Rather than insulting Joe with my prediction, I have praised his character, and praiseworthiness and blameworthiness are the necessary pillars supporting the free will concept. If I said that although I have known Joe for years, he is a free autonomous agent, and therefore I do not know if he will turn it in, I would be insulting his moral character by implying that he may decide not to.

Free Will as Quantitative

Although I accept soft determinism, I disavow hard determinism. If human action was just the result of pre-existing determinative forces, desire and motive would translate into action with the lubricated ease of a Rolls Royce engine, but it does not. Choices are burdensome; they must often be made against the gravitational pull of impulse, habit, convention, sloth, and the presence of many alternative options. We often make bad choices, recognized only as such by hindsight, when all we can do is resolve not to make them again. That is what free will is supposed to be; the ability to make both good and bad choices and to be determined to learn from them. Even as we acknowledge that factors impinging on our life choices have significance, they are still subject to our appraisal as to how we may deal with them constructively. I also disavow absolute libertarian free will because we are subject to cause and effect. No human being can have absolute free will, for it is impossible to be entirely self-determined.

I find neuroscientist Bjorn Brembs' (2011, p. 933) position on free will to be congenial. Brembs views free will as a quantitative trait with some having more of it than others: "A scientific concept of free will cannot be a qualitative concept. The question is not any more 'do we have free will?' [but rather] 'how much free will do we have'?" By conceptualizing free will/agency as a quantitative rather than a qualitative binary either/or thing, it is logical to assume that we become increasingly freer of external constraints as we move from childhood to old age. Being freer of external constraints means that we are able to live progressively more in accordance with the proclivities of our natures leavened by the wisdom of age. Behavioral genetic studies consistently and robustly find that as we age the influences of shared environments (in which we are under the considerable control of others—parent, teachers, and so forth) on our personalities, cognitive abilities, and behavior fade to almost nothing while the influence of genes (which belong to us) and non-shared environments (which we partly create by interacting with the environment in ways that accord with our personalities) become stronger (van Drunen et al., 2021; Walters, 2022). The old saying is true: "The older I get, the more I become myself."

This notion is somewhat akin to Sartre's concept of existence preceding essence. Sartre reasoned that only designed material objects such as hammers and automobiles have an essence prior to their existence because they were designed with their "essential" functions built in. Humans were not created for a purpose like hammers or automobiles; they simply find themselves existing and must devise their own purpose for being. For Sartre, one's life has no *a priori* meaning, and one must choose one's own meaning and purpose in life. Sartre considered it wrong to treat human beings in the same way we treat things created for a purpose since he maintained that there is no universal human nature, or essence, in the same sense as hammers or automobiles have essential qualities. As Dilman (2013) describes Sartre's position,

> We see that when Sartre claims that man is inescapably and absolutely free he is repudiating causal determination in an original way by making a fundamental distinction and a radical break between man, in the character of his existence, and the rest of nature. This is reminiscent of Kant's distinction between the world of phenomena in which causality reigns supreme and the world of noumena or intelligibilia, or even of significances, in which the will, at one with reason, is autonomous and, therefore, free. Both Kant and Sartre knew, of course, that man is not always autonomous and that autonomy is something which man achieves. (Dilman, 2013, p. 192)

Sartre's claim is that what humans become is determined (if he will excuse my use of the term) by choices made by their inescapable free will. There is a responsibility that goes with those choices, but free will allows them to refuse to shoulder this responsibility. Not accepting the responsibility to achieve autonomy amounts to self-deception, which Sartre called "bad faith." Although in some respects I find this view agreeable, I find it too libertarian. There is a universal human nature "designed" by natural selection, and therefore an "essence" that distinguishes humanity from everything not sharing that nature. Indeed, Rigoni et al. (2012, pp. 1482–1483) maintain that evolution has provided us with a free-willed brain to deal with behavioral variability: "Evolution would have shaped the brain to produce behavioral variability, and this variability would not be predictable. Free will would then be an intrinsic characteristic of the brain." If human beings in all cultures at all times did not have the same nature —that is, the same hopes, aspirations, character traits, emotions, feelings, goals, needs, moral strengths, and weaknesses—it would be difficult to grasp the wisdom bequeathed to us by the past. We understand Antigone's struggles with King Creon; Plato's allegories resonate so strongly with us today; we appreciate Odysseus' struggle for self-identity and Penelope's patient and faithful love; and military leaders and businessmen the world over have found wisdom in Sun-Tzu's *Art of War*, written in 6th-century BC China. To the extent that humans can become autonomous agents, however, I wholeheartedly agree with Sartre that it is incumbent on us to strive toward autonomy and not to succumb to making bad faith excuses for our poor choices.

Free Mind

What does it mean to have a free mind, and how is that distinguished from free will? Take the romance of Romeo and Juliette. Both had the desire to mate hard-wired into their wills in a generalized form we call erotic desire. So, the *ultimate* cause of their romance was nature's sole concern, that of the continuance of life. But that can be achieved by any appropriate coupling of opposite sexes. What was it about Juliette that attracted Romeo and led him to focus his desire exclusively on her? What was going on in his mind that made him love her so intensely that he would die for her, which in fact he did? We can talk about the hormone of lust (testosterone), the neurochemicals of romantic love (dopamine, serotonin, and norepinephrine), and of attachment (oxytocin and vasopressin), but these are just the biochemical tools love makes use of, and not the emotion that Shakespeare called "winged cupid painted blind." To say that Romeo had no choice but to fall in love with Juliette and that love is reducible to, and determined by, a reductionist "bottom-up" neurochemistry is to mock common sense. After all, he did choose her over Rosaline, and when he did his neurochemistry *responded* appropriately by translating the abstract language of his mind to the material language of his brain. All purposeful human actions evidence this "top-down" pattern of causality—we chose and our brains provide the required substances to make our choices transpire.

German philosopher Arthur Schopenhauer's words lead us to differentiate between free will and free mind: "Man can do what he wants, but he cannot will what he wills" (in Clark, 2007, p. 96). In other words, absent constraints, we are free to do whatever our wills desire, but we are not free to choose what we desire because we are acting in accordance with inner necessity—in accordance with our natures. Likewise, we are not free to choose wants that run contrary to our natures—that is, wants that would disgust, harm, or terrorize us. To say that we can will absolutely anything, including things contrary to our nature, is to think of free-willed actions as entirely capricious and probabilistically unpredictable, which, to quote Max Weber again, is the "privilege of the insane."

In the Schopenhauerian sense, "will" has a different meaning than its meaning in "free will," but it stands closer in many ways to the notion that our wills initiate movement toward desired goals. Schopenhauer is saying that our conscious choices are driven by subconscious desires that emanate from our shared human nature, our unique genetic endowment, and the learned habits of our lives. These are the things that lead us to "will" (desire) certain things and courses of action over others. This may not be considered free will in the libertarian sense, but it does not make a real practical difference when we apply it to the meaningful choices people make when multiple options engage multiple desires vying for supremacy.

Even for mundane everyday choices, if the choice is between two options congenial to one's nature, one will follow the strongest inclination. We are thus free only to follow our strongest inclination. I see no problem with this kind of freedom. After all, my strongest inclination is *my* strongest inclination, and no one else's. My nature is me and my will is mine, and if I follow the direction my nature nudges me in pursuit of my goals, I am following my will. If I am free to follow the dictates of my nature, and at the same time free to ignore them, then I am as free as it is logically possible to be because the dictates moving me are mine and mine alone. To ask for freedom beyond that is meaningless; how can one be free of one's nature? Free will is ultimately the uniquely human ability to take ownership of our natural desires and control them. Humans have the ability to actively reflect on their desires to form judgments concerning their desirability in light of many other moral and pragmatic considerations. If a person is saddled with a malevolent nature and refuses to shoulder the responsibility of controlling their base desires, then there are prisons awaiting them.

Even though there are people who are slaves to their natural desires, this does not mean that such desires are bad. They are part of what it means to be human, but Sartre would say that we have veto power over them and should not follow them to immoral excess. We are free to forego the exercise of natural desires, as do priests, nuns, and monks who vow to forego earthly pleasures to follow the religious life. These people (in general) defy the most urgent human desires when they consciously and deliberately chose chastity and poverty over sexual pleasure and material comforts. Does anyone believe that they could not have chosen otherwise? One could still argue, of course, that they were following a strong inclination inspired by beliefs planted in their minds by others, and that they felt a call from God to follow the spiritual path of life. But those beliefs and feelings are abstractions of the mind and have no palpable material substance as the promise of the pleasures of the flesh do. The metaphysical mind thus won the battle between tangible desires or inclinations. In his hierarchic theory of free will, neuroscientist T. T. Hills explains this by distinguishing between first-order desires and second-order volitions and notes that "second-order volitions have preferences over first-order desires. Theories that involve a consistent mapping among a hierarchy of desires are called mesh theories. They claim that when desires at different levels in the cognitive system 'mesh' in a harmonious way, then the person acts unimpeded; her actions and the desires or intentions causing them are a free outcome of her exercising her own agency" (2019, p. 4).

Thus, in the Schopenhauerian sense, it is not the will (desires) that is free, but the agent's mind that is free to choose how, why, or when natural desires are sought, and to what extent, or to forego them all together in favor of abstract beliefs and feelings that have little or no purchase for most people. Conscious rational deliberation—free mind—is arguably the key to limited human freedom because it can break the chain initiated by the desires of the will at any point. If the will is to be free, it requires a free mind. If we do not have free will (free mind), why do we all, including those who deny it, act as though we do? We acquire the notion that we are free agents, albeit with boundaries, through the everyday experience of our own volition. Surely, we could not fabricate the idea of free will without a basis for it in the reality of everyday experience. Having said that, it is doubtless true that our sense of free will exceeds our actual capacity to act autonomously.

We cannot prove free will by scientific means, but the issue could be resolved by demonstrating its nonexistence. The only way we could do this would be with models of different kinds of human behavior that allow us to predict those behaviors with almost 100% accuracy, or at least models that account for almost all the statistical variance in the behavior we are hoping to predict. As we saw earlier, even the most inclusive models we have at present cannot even reach 50% accuracy in their predictions. We are thus left with three choices (if hard determinists will excuse my use of that word): we can trust our perceptions that we have free will with boundaries, we can deny that we have such a bounded free will despite the absence of solid evidence for that position, or we can be agnostic on the issue.

Free will skeptics talk the talk, but do they walk the walk in their own lives? If people cannot do otherwise than they do, do skeptics no longer praise people's accomplishments, or blame them for their malfeasance? If someone helps them out of a dilemma and someone else cuckolds them, does the free will skeptic dismiss the former's aid as inevitable and excuse the latter's iniquity as unavoidable consequences of predetermined causes? If they are like you and me, they are very grateful in the first instance and as mad as hell in the second, and thus free will skeptics do not swallow their own medicine and are walking, talking, thinking self-contradictions.

Chapter Two

Brain/Mind Duality and Consciousness

Is There an Ontological and Epistemic Distinction Between Brain and Mind?

Closely related to the free will/determinism issue is the issue of how the immaterial mind and the material brain relate to one another (Georgiev, 2020). The human brain is without a doubt evolution's magnum opus, the most complicated and fascinating entity in the universe. Nobel laureate physicist Roger Penrose has said: "If you look at the entire physical cosmos, our brains are a tiny, tiny, part of it. But they're the most perfectly organized part. Compared to the complexity of a brain, a galaxy is just an inert lump" (in Holt, 2012, p. 178). Nobel laureate neuroscientist Roger Sperry augments this: "In the human head there are forces within forces within forces, as in no other cubic half–foot of the universe we know" (in Fincher, 1982, p. 23). Although the brain constitutes only 2% of body mass, about 50 to 60% of our genes are involved in building it, and it consumes a voracious 20% of the body's energy resources (Mitchell, 2007). Genes build brains, but the building is more complex than the builder. Humans have far too few genes (about 22,000) to determine the function of our brains, which involves trillions of synaptic connections.

We could exhaust a whole dictionary of sparkling metaphors to sing the praises of this enchanted loom, because within its chemical soup and electrical sparks lie our thoughts, memories, desires, emotions, intelligence, and creativity. We could deduce from this that these electrochemicals shunting around molecules in the brain fully account for our conscious deliberations in reductionist bottom-up fashion, but no one has the slightest idea how anything material like the brain could be conscious of itself. Eliminative materialism relegates the conscious mind to brain activity with no independent existence, "a computer made of meat," as some neuroscientists like to call it. They say this because thoughts cannot occur without the brain and because they can change brain states by stimulating neurons or administering drugs and other substances. But there is a bridge between neural connections and mental space, and it is crossed in both directions. Of course, we can have a brain without a mind, but we cannot have a mind without a brain any more than we can see without eyes. While this is true, there is a growing literature affirming that the conscious mind exists as an abstract entity separate from the brain, although the brain is its platform.

The idea that the mind and body are distinct entities with different essential qualities is known as mind/brain dualism. It is an ancient notion, but the most well-known version is credited to the 17th-century French physician, philosopher, and mathematician Rene Descartes. According to Descartes, we can doubt anything except that we doubt, and doubting is thinking. Thus, the only thing we can be absolutely certain of is that we think, as his famous dictum asserts: "*Cogito ergo sum*" (I think, therefore I am). For Descartes, the body is an extended (it occupies space) material unthinking thing subject to mechanical laws, while the mind is an un-extended (it transcends space) immaterial thing that thinks, and is not subject to mechanical laws (Descartes, de Spinoza, & Hutchins, 1952).

This is not a view shared by most neuroscientists, because the mind does not have form or occupy space. However, David Chalmers, who has perhaps researched and written more on consciousness than any other scientist alive, argues that the conscious mind does not logically depend entirely on the brain, and thus cannot be reduced to it. Instead, he argues that the immaterial conscious mind supervenes on the material brain in some unknown way. He writes: "I resisted mind-body dualism for a long time, but I have now come to the point where I accept it, not just as the only tenable view but as a satisfying view in its own right. ... I can comfortably say that I think dualism is very likely true" (1996, p. 357).

Biophysicist Danko Georgiev (2020) appeals to anesthetized brains to argue for dualism:

> Apparently, the mind and the brain are not identical, because anesthetized brains do not generate conscious experiences. In the course of general anesthesia consciousness is erased by the pharmacological action of the anesthetic drug, yet the experimenter may stimulate with visible light the open eyes of anesthetized animals and still evoke electric potentials by pyramidal neurons located in the primary visual cortex. … If mind states were related to brain states through one-to-one correspondence (logical identity relation), it should not have been possible to turn mental states on or off using general anesthetics, because the brain states would have always remained mental states. Thus, the mind/brain problem is to explain how the unobservable conscious mind and the observable brain relate to each other: do they interact or does one unilaterally generate the other? (Georgiev, 2020, p. 17)

The configurations of our brain states occur in top-down fashion in response to our goals, beliefs, and desires in a way not captured by bottom-up mechanistic descriptions. Recall our discussion of the brain chemistry involved in the experience of love. Reductionist accounts describe what goes on in the brain *after* people are in love; in no way is it a description of *why* they are in love. The relevance of the product of brain activity for every lover is not mechanistic; the relevance is the information in their minds about what each represents to the other. I am thrilled with the windows into the mind that neuroscience has provided, but disturbed by the price we pay for transcribing the mind onto chemicals and tissue without remainder. Abstract mental and physical brain events are intimately connected, but to say that the former is *nothing but* a function of the latter is illogical. Just as your car gets you to the next town without making you go there, so does your brain facilitate your mental journeys without making you take them. By itself—when your mind is not at the wheel—the brain can only take you into dark places.

It is often asserted that our abstract minds are simply epiphenomena of our physical brains. For instance, Nobel laureate Francis Crick has written: "'You,' your joys and your sorrows, your memories and your ambitions, your sense of personal identity and free will, are in fact no more than the behavior of a vast assembly of nerve cells and their associated molecules. Who you are is nothing but a pack of neurons" (1994, p. 3). If Crick is going to travel this reductionist route, he might have gone further because neurons are made of atoms, and atoms are made of even smaller particles, so he might have said that we are nothing but a pack of quarks. Mental phenomena require the brain as its physical platform, but the mind cannot be reduced to it without remainder. Crick's reductionist words come from his book *The Astonishing Hypothesis.* It is indeed astonishing, and one wonders why he didn't subtitle it *The Zombie Within.*

Our brains allow us to function as free volitional agents by providing the physical mechanisms by which we emote, think, believe, desire, and plan. Our minds instigate these things, and the brain responds and facilitates them by engaging those mechanisms. All human actions require a rational mind that forms intentions and an acting agent to carry them out. The contents of the mind use the brain to form intentions, and physical brain states reflect those intentions. It is the mind that exercises causal agency; we pick up a spade to dig a hole or strike a computer key to make a letter, all at the instigation of mind, and our extended bodies are the instruments by which we accomplish such tasks. Just as the lungs exist so that we may breathe, the brain exists so that we may "mind."

Studies of London taxi drivers provide compelling evidence of the brain's ability to transform itself in response to mental activity. London cab drivers have to constantly learn new routes in a city of over 600 square miles with streets laid out in a spaghetti-like snarl. Using functional magnetic resonance imaging (fMRI), researchers find that cab drivers have significantly larger hippocampi (the organs of memory) than Londoners employed in other working-class occupations, and the longer they had been employed as cab drivers, the larger these structures are found to be (Woollett & Maguire, 2011). If mental activity changes brain structures, perhaps it is not that the mind is "just the brain at work," but rather that the brain is "just the mind at work." When we think of a mathematical equation, a musical score, or a philosophical argument, it is the meaning we ascribe to those thoughts that are fundamental, not the neural substrates recruited to make the meaning possible. It is the mind that organizes the bombardment of external stimuli that gives meaning to the brain's physical activity. The brain cannot bootstrap itself into meaningful activity by purely internal processes; it must interact with information content from outside itself in a reciprocal causal way.

Mind and Information

How do we define a mind except to say that it is the abstract "something" with which we think? This may not be a satisfactory definition since we have defined it only in terms of what it does—move concepts, problems, perceptions, and so on around in our heads. It is a tautology akin to the standard definition of energy as the "capacity to do work." You can't see, touch, weigh, or smell energy; it is an intangible "something" only indirectly observed as it moves physical things around. Despite its centrality to physics, Nobel laureate Richard Feynman tells us that "It is important to realize that in physics today, we have no knowledge of what energy is" (in Hecht, 2007, p. 88). To be sure, it is more represented in mathematical terms by which we can make useful predictions and is quantified in joules, calories, kilowatts, and so on, than mind, but its essence, what it actually "is," still eludes us. One may argue, of course, that we quantify the mind similarly with IQ tests and personality inventories.

It is useful to think of mental phenomena as we think of DNA—as information. Mental information is stored in the neural structures of the brain just as biological information is stored in DNA. In their packaged form, both are temporarily "material," or at least materially housed. When our thoughts are communicated outward to other minds, they are converted from their material substrate to a form of immaterial energy. When stored by self or other, they are again embodied in matter. Think of this as analogous to writing on a computer. When I write at my computer, what I intend to say precedes the electrical patterns engaged within the computer, and then my thoughts become physically manifested on the screen and are stored in the electrical entrails of the computer. The information content of my thoughts is obviously not determined by the electrical patterns within the computer, although I need the computer (or some other physical medium) to make my thoughts manifest. My thoughts precede these electrical patterns like Romeo's love preceded the soup and sparks of his brain when he fell for Juliette, and are thus not caused by those patterns. When I decide which keys to hit to make manifest the thoughts that "come to mind," a specific sequence of electrical activity is fired up within the computer; thus, my immaterial mind has acted causally on a material object. Moreover, when I wrote these words, I excluded all other word possibilities from being actualized. That is, I freely chose to write "this" as opposed to "that," and this constitutes my mind's freedom to create verbal reality out of mere possibility.

As with the electrical entrails of my computer, I act causally on the activity of my brain when I think. When I wrote this sentence I "fired up" a specific sequence of electrochemical activity in my brain, which corresponded to the neural correlates of my mind. If I change my mind to form a different sentence, a different sequence of neuronal firing takes place. This is top-down causation by which physical events in my brain are caused by my mind. That is, the thoughts in my mind caused a particular sequence of neural firing and not vice versa. Every mind state becomes a brain state, but mental properties are not entirely reducible to neural properties. Nobel laureate neuroscientist and surgeon Sir John Eccles supports this view: "The more we discover scientifically about the brain the more clearly do we distinguish between the brain events and the mental phenomena and the more wonderful do the mental phenomena become. There is a fundamental mystery in my personal existence, transcending the biological account of the development of my body and my brain" (in Brian, 1995, p. 371).

Nobel laureate physicist Eugene Wigner is vexed by eliminative reductionism to the material. He opines that quantum physics renders strict materialistic causality logically inconsistent with the mind: "one may well wonder how materialism, the doctrine that 'life could be explained by sophisticated combinations of physical and chemical laws,' could so long be accepted by the majority of scientists. The reason is probably that it is an emotional necessity to exalt the problem to which one wants to devote a lifetime" (2013, p. 177). Writing of the awesome intellect of the great mathematicians, Wigner notes: "certainly it is hard to believe that our reasoning power was brought, by the Darwinian process of natural selection, to the perfection which it seems to possess" (1990, p. 3). Stressing the complexity of the mathematics involved in quantum mechanics, he adds: "It is difficult to avoid the impression that a miracle confronts us here quite comparable in its striking nature to the miracle that the human mind can string a thousand arguments together without getting itself into contradictions or the two miracles of the existence of the laws of nature and of the human mind's capacity to divine them" (1990, p. 7).

Consciousness

How did we acquire a mind capable of such complex abstract reasoning? How did this lump of mushy tissue acquire the capacity to be aware that it exists, inject meaning into its circuitry, and the intellectual power to probe itself? In other words, how did we acquire consciousness? Consciousness is a mental state of awareness of one's objective and subjective experiences and of one's *intentional* ability to manipulate and fashion those experiences and to inject meaning into them. This is simple enough to say, but many who have thought deeply on the subject aver that consciousness is *the* most difficult problem with which psychologists and neuroscientists have to wrestle. For instance, Kauffman and Radin (2021, p. 1) opine: "Of the three central mysteries in science, the Origin of the Universe, the Origin of Life, and the Origin of Consciousness, the last is the most challenging." We have theories of consciousness, but Chalmers (1996) writes: "Most existing theories of consciousness either deny the phenomenon, explain something else, or elevate the problem to an eternal mystery" (p. 217). In another forum, Chalmers maintains that the task before neuroscientists "is to build a nonreductive account of consciousness, one that does not attempt to reduce consciousness to something else, but which admits it as an irreducible feature of the world" (2017, p. 234).

But why should consciousness be such a perversely difficult problem when nothing is more obvious than the fact that we are conscious? As obvious as its existence is, consciousness is so difficult to define because it is abstract and operates mysteriously. The difficulty of the problem lies in explaining a neurological basis of consciousness since as an immaterial abstraction it is a part of reality that cannot be reduced to physics and chemistry. This is anathema to the eliminative materialist notion that only material exists, so the best way out is to consider consciousness an illusion, as Daniel Dennett has said: "It's the brain's 'user illusion' of itself" (in Buckley, 2017, np). Nobel laureate physicist Robert Millikan, however, views consciousness as quite real and a great gift: "The most amazing thing in all life, the greatest miracle there is, is the fact that a mind has got here at all, 'created out of the dust of the earth.' This is the Bible phrase, and science today can find no better way to describe it—a mind" (1927, p. 69).

Strict materialism offers no real alternative except to say this highest manifestation of life is just a strange coincidence that we must simply accept as a brute fact. Witness Stephen Jay Gould's statement: "Consciousness, vouchsafed only to our species in the history of life on earth, is the most god-awfully potent evolutionary invention ever developed. Although accidental and unpredictable, it has given *Homo sapiens* unprecedented power both over the history of our own species and the life of the entire contemporary biosphere" (1997, p. ix). How could Gould's accident have occurred when evolution's sole "purpose" is the continued existence of life? Natural selection is a winnowing process that selects only those alleles that contribute to the twin goals of survival and reproduction. This being the case, all humans would need to survive and reproduce the instincts that further these goals, just like all other animal species.

Humans possess these instincts, so why add a conscious mind to the human repertoire when the rest of animal life follows the evolutionary imperative without it? Adding mind would seem to be an impediment to reproductive success since humans generally seek mating opportunities with moral rules that prevent them from seizing every opportunity that presents itself. It is difficult to see evolutionary pressures being exerted to gift us with an impediment to biological fitness. Some neuroscientists believe that consciousness emerged from the increasing complexity of social life and that the need to navigate more social relationships led to a bigger brain (Muthukrishna et al., 2018), but brain size does not inform us about the issue of consciousness. The human brain is much bigger relative to body size than is necessary to fulfill the Darwinian imperative, and it is energetically costly to maintain (Bordone et al., 2019). Much brain energy is expended appreciating abstract reasoning in mathematics and science, and in the creation and appreciation of music, art, and the beauty of the world. This is a wonderful gift as Wigner says, "we neither understand nor deserve," but it does not afford our species any fitness advantage in raw Darwinian terms, so we should not have such a marvelous "illogical" gift. Physicist John Polkinghorne likewise notes that "Human powers of rational comprehension vastly exceed anything that could be simply an evolutionary necessity for survival, or plausibly construed of some sort of collateral spinoff from such a necessity" (in Frankenberry, 2008, p. 345).

Gould says above that consciousness is unique to our species, but all animals have a rudimentary form of consciousness. They are aware of dangers, food and water sources, and mating opportunities, but they are not aware that they are aware. As purely instinctual beings, they are constrained to act in accordance with their genes. They are adapted to their environments, but they cannot create them. Because humans have a mind, they have escaped the captivity of mere instinctive responses to sensory perceptions. We enjoy an inner world that demands that we impose order on the content of our sensory perceptions and think above and beyond them. Humans actively create their environments, rather than merely adapt to them, through their ability to think rationally and to communicate their thoughts to others. Language is a powerful externalizer of our thoughts, and the words that give them voice can powerfully influence others, for good or ill. Animals are able to communicate their intentions through sounds and gestures, but such communication is a far cry from the fine nuances of language.

Fine-Tuning the Brain

The physical brain is the mind's home, and a "quality" brain allows for a quality prosocial mind. Whatever one's position on mind/brain duality is, it is incontrovertible that a well-functioning brain is essential for living one's life in ways that comport with decency, responsibility, self-efficacy, and well-being. Because our experiences, especially in early childhood, are physically captured by the brain by the process of synaptogenesis, experiencing joy and acceptance in love from others sets us on a firm path. Love is the junction where our discussions of criminality, brain, mind, and consciousness meet and merge. Many criminals were deprived of love growing up, so their mental representations of the world are not prosocial. TenHouten (2021, p. 713) writes of criminals in maximum-security U.S. prisons, and dramatically states: "without either the experiences of, and capacity, for love, and especially for self-love, 'the self collapses, the soul dies, [and] the psyche goes to hell.' These men strive to protect themselves from the reality of having being deprived of love by emptying their souls of love for others, and a soul empty of love fills with hatred."

Love is a mysteriously powerful force—the noblest, most beautiful, exquisite, and meaningful experience of humanity. By love we are born, through it we are sustained, and for it we may sacrifice life itself. Love insulates the child, brings joy to youth, and provides comfort and sustenance to the aged. Its boundless power cures the sick, raises the fallen, and comforts the tormented. It is the magnetism between man and woman, the unending devotion of parents for their children, and the active concern for the well-being of our fellow human beings. Giving and receiving love is imperative for the meaningful lives of human beings, and those that can neither give nor receive it walk in darkness.

Mothers are our first environment; first in the womb and then at the breast. Mother love is not *eros*—the kind of love that depends upon the lovable qualities of the beloved, but rather *agape*, a selfless "giving" love rooted purely in the relationship between the lover and the loved. A mother's love for the issue of her womb is not rooted in their children's virtue or in their just desserts, but rather in selfless *agape* rooted in the knowledge that the creature in her arms is her child. A father's love is somewhat different but complementary. In a general sense, mothers make their children *capable* of love, and fathers take this capacity and cultivate it through the inculcation of the ideals of humanity to make them *worthy* of love (Fromm, 1956). Of course, mothers' agape and fathers' eros overlap; they are not mutually exclusive; they just signify different male or female tendencies that are both needed. This is why growing up without the presence of a father, as do so many criminals, is a disaster that may foreclose their efforts to become authentic human beings in the Sartrean sense and leads to so many "bad faith" choices.

The physical manifestations of mother love are important because human infants are born with highly underdeveloped brains relative to other species, and much human brain development occurs outside the womb (Ouyang et al., 2019). Newborn mammals of other species can walk within hours or days and can fend for themselves not long thereafter. Human babies do not typically walk until about one year old, and they certainly cannot take care of themselves for years. This is why the experience of loving nurturing is required during the earliest periods of synaptogenesis. Experience alters the adult brain, but it literally organizes the infant's (Tooley, Bassett, & Mackey, 2021). The warm tactile and olfactory sensations of breastfeeding and being kissed and cuddled send signals through the infant's brain running to its pleasure centers that calibrate the plastic brain and tells the infant that all is right with its world. At this stage of life, the infant can only "think" with its skin, and its mother is the fountainhead of all its satisfactions.

Affectionate touching, kissing, cuddling, and hugging are tangible assurances for the infant that it is loved and all is right with its world, an attitude that in all likelihood will last a lifetime. A mother's touch communicates her loving emotions and sends signals of security to her infant because the neural tube is formed from the same embryonic tissue (the ectoderm) making the skin and the brain intimately connected (Dias & Partington, 2015). We know that the more infants are picked up and stroked, the more abundant the synaptic connections available for selection (Mayford, Siegelbaum, & Kandel, 2012). The synapses selected for retention are those most frequently and strongly made, whether they are made in response to either positive or negative experiences. This is why loving tactile stimulation is so important for an infant's healthy brain (and thus, mind) development, why most mothers have the desire to provide it, and why both receive joy in the process. The expansion of two individual natures by love is achieved in this fashion, each enriching and being enriched by the other.

This is all very deterministic, but it is not a problem because we have noted that free will (or free mind) operates in a deterministic world and the validity of the free mind concept does not hinge on the question of scientific determinism. Having worked in the criminal justice field for a number of years, I am well aware that many criminals are born to drug-addicted and/or alcoholic mothers who do not provide the kinds of loving interactions described above. Furthermore, most of our worst criminals grew up in father-absent homes, as Edward Kruk notes:

> Eighty-five percent of youth in prison have an absent father, 71% of high school dropouts are fatherless, 90% of homeless and runaway children have an absent father, and fatherless children and youth exhibit higher levels of depression and suicide, delinquency, promiscuity and teen pregnancy, behavioral problems and illicit and licit substance abuse, diminished self-concepts, and are more likely to be victims of exploitation and abuse. (2012, p. 49)

According to James Q. Wilson, to focus on father-absence as conducive to crime "is to risk being called a racist, unless you quickly add that families are not important to children, in which case you may be called either a progressive or a fool" (2000, p. 107). But African American activists

Cosby and Poussaint agree: “A house without a father is a challenge. A neighborhood without fathers is a catastrophe” (2007, p. 3). Even burdened by a bad early environment, people are not robbed of their bounded free will or of their rational understanding of what is right and what is wrong. Millions of people have survived abysmal early environments to become productive law-abiding citizens, and deserve praise for having done so. We assign moral responsibility to criminals because they are human beings and therefore have a free mind and consciousness of wrongdoing unless they have some form of mental disease or defect that are pathologies of the will. To state otherwise is to deprive them of their humanity and reduce them to beasts of burden. Criminals’ conscious avoidance of their responsibility to behave lawfully (Sartre’s bad faith) calls down upon their own heads the punishment they receive even though we can articulate understandable reasons for their poor choices.

Chapter Three

Behavioral Genetics: Genes and Free Will

Genetic Determinism

Psychologist Roy Baumeister notes that "Many psychologists disdain the idea of free will, for several reasons. First, some think that in order to be a scientist it is necessary to believe in determinism, because a scientist studies causality and cannot tolerate or accept exceptions. Second, and related to the first, free choice (especially the full, extreme case of total freedom) cannot seem to be explained in scientific terms" (2008, p. 15). It is not just psychologists, but perhaps most social scientists disavow free will in the wish to be thought of as solid empirical scientists. Yet when it comes to talk about genes and human traits and actions, "determinism" becomes a pejorative term. As one who has been involved in biosocial criminology most of my career, I have lost count of the number of times I have heard the phrase "genetic determinism" describe its agenda. Those who make the accusation don't like it but fear it to be true.

Except in rare cases of diseases such as Huntington's chorea, no geneticist accepts genetic determinism, so why do so many social scientists (although the number is dwindling as the biosocial perspective has gained traction in many disciplines) think there is such an animal? Jamieson and Radick (2017) maintain that the notion goes back to the limited understanding of genetics obtained in Biology 101. If we took that course, we learned that genes have alternate forms called alleles that occupy the same locus on a particular chromosome. Using Gregor Mendel's peas as the iconic example, the professor placed these alleles in Punnett squares (big T for tall, little t for short, big S for smooth, little s for wrinkled) and demonstrated that if a pea plant had TtSs alleles, its immutable destiny was to be tall and smooth. If we think that genes work this way in forming the contours of human personality and behavior, it is understandable that it makes many of those whose knowledge of genetics ended with bio 101 nervous.

Nature and nurture are intertwined, but genetic determinism implies that human personality and social behavior are *direct* outcomes of genes absent any influence from the environment or from human agency. Such reasoning "represents either mere rhetoric or simple ignorance. No evolutionary psychologist [nor biosocial criminologist, geneticist, or neuroscientist] doubts that a gene is in constant dialogue with its surroundings, which include the other genes in the genome, the rest of the organism, and the world at large" (Trudge, 1999, p. 96). Matt Ridley has some astute observations about genetic determinism for those who fear its existence:

> Genes are not puppet masters, nor blueprints. They may direct the construction of the body and brain in the womb, but they set about dismantling and rebuilding what they have made almost at once *in response to experience*. They are both the cause and consequence of our actions. Somehow the adherents of the "nurture" side of the argument have scared themselves silly at the power and inevitability of genes, and missed the greatest lesson of all: *the genes are on our side.* (2003, p. 6; emphasis added)

These are truisms of genetics; the genome is a reactive system rather than a controlling system. The genome receives signals from the environment that activate transcription factors that lead to neurotransmitter and hormonal activity that enable us to effectively respond to whatever circumstance (including our conscious intentions) activated those signals. Thus, genes are at our beck and call, not we at theirs. Nevertheless, genes are an important link in the chain influencing our personality traits and behaviors, as has been amply demonstrated by thousands of behavioral genetic studies. These studies may appear deterministic at first blush because they rarely, if ever, engage philosophically with the free will/determinism issue because such is not in their purview. However, evolutionary scientist Christopher Badcock (2000, p. 71) opines that our genes "positively guarantee" human freedom, and neurobiologist Steven Rose (2001, p. 6) writes: "Individually and collectively we have the ability our own futures, albeit in circumstances not of our own choosing. Thus, it is that our biology makes us free."

The Concept of Heritability

Behavioral genetics is the science that seeks to understand the genetic and environmental sources of individual trait and behavioral variation. These sources, along with measurement error, account for 100% of the variation, but we can find volitional choice hiding in there if we look. Heritability (h^2) is a quantification ranging between 0 and 1 of the extent to which variance in a trait is attributable to genes in a particular population and is calculated via the formula: $h^2 = 2(rMZ - rDZ)$. That is, h^2 is equal to twice the difference between the monozygotic (MZ) and dizygotic (DZ) twin pair correlations for a given variable. It is a *population* parameter that apportions trait variance averaged over all subjects into genetic and environmental sources, and its values depend on environmental quality. Behavioral genetic analyses are about *variation* in traits or behaviors in a particular population, in a particular environment, at a particular time; they cannot inform us which genes influence our traits or behaviors, but tell us the extent to which people in a particular population differ genetically with respect to those traits and behaviors.

All cognitive, behavioral, and personality traits are heritable, which led Turkheimer (2000) to posit that $h^2 \neq 0$ be enshrined as the first law of behavioral genetics. A meta-analysis of 2,748 twin studies published over 50 years using more than 14.5 million twin pairs from 39 different countries showed that all human traits are heritable (Polderman et al., 2015). Heritability coefficients of around 0.50 have been calculated for such unlikely features as divorce and political ideology, which tends to make those unfamiliar with the logic of behavioral genetics want to dismiss it. Of course, there are no "divorce" or "political ideology" genes any more than there are "crime genes." What h^2 captures is a variety of genes that, in concert with the way they interact with their environments, make an outcome more likely than not. People who are difficult to get along with, are unwilling to compromise, and/or find it difficult to remain faithful are more likely to get divorced than people with the opposite heritable traits (Hatemi, McDermott, & Eaves, 2015). It is those traits that are "in" the genes, not divorce per se. Likewise, our temperaments tend to make some people view the political world *primarily* through their feelings and other people *primarily* via more intellectual analysis (Walsh, 2022).

This is similar to the effect of genes on antisocial behavior. A meta-analysis of 28,709 sibling pairs in 103 twin and adoption studies revealed that 58% of the total phenotypic variance in antisocial behavior is accounted for by genes (Burt, 2009). Criminality, like divorce or political ideology, is a complex phenotype consisting of a number of endophenotypes (within the phenotype). Endophenotypes are parts of the complex chain leading from genotype (in concert with the environment and the choices people make) to phenotype, but each of them may have only minor effects on the phenotype, and then only if combined with other relevant endophenotypes and the right circumstances. Reducing the criminality phenotype to its constituent endophenotypes such as impulsiveness or low empathy makes it easier to identify their genetic basis because intermediate traits (the endophenotypes) "sit closer to the genotype in the development scheme" (Gottesman & Hanson, 2005, p. 268).

There are two ways in which behavioral geneticists examine environmental and genetic influences on a trait: adoption and twin studies. Adoption studies are "natural experiments" that randomize genes (twins adopted into different families) to investigate the effect of shared environments and randomize environments to investigate the effect of shared genes. To the extent that genetically unrelated individuals reared in the same home display trait similarities, they must be entirely a function of shared environment, and similarities between genetically related individuals reared apart must be entirely a function of shared genes. The correlation between twin pairs reared apart is a straightforward indication of heritability since there is no shared environment, and the correlation between unrelated individuals reared in the same home is a straightforward measure of shared environment effects since they share no genes.

Twin studies rely on comparisons of interclass correlations for a trait between MZ twin pairs and same-sex DZ twin pairs to sort out genetic and environmental sources of trait variance. MZ twins are genetically identical, that is, they share 100% of their genes, and DZ twins share an average of 50% of their genes. It follows that the more genes that pairs of individuals have in common, the more similar they should be on phenotypic traits. Behavioral genetic studies are not perfect, but they provide unparalleled precision in researching human personality and behavior. Purely environmental research could only achieve the same level of precision if we were to "have 'identical environmental twins' whose experiences were exactly the same, moment by moment, and another variety [DZ twins] who shared exactly but randomly [as they share randomly 50% of their genes] 50% of their experiences" (Turkheimer, 2000, p. 162). There are no environmental twins, but they are not needed because behavior genetics informs us of the environmental contribution to human traits as surely as if there were because $1.0 - h^2$ is the proportion of phenotypic variance attributable to the environment.

Heritability is the proportion of variance in a trait attributable to *actualized* genetic potential in a population; we cannot infer from it what the unactualized potential may be. Determining heritability requires that every phenotype be exposed to identical developmental environments because variation can only be attributed to factors that vary. If we took a random sample of genetically heterogeneous tomato seeds and planted them in identically nourishing environments, phenotypic trait variance would be *entirely* attributable to genetics ($h^2 = 1.0$). Because the environment was held constant, it cannot be considered a source of variance in their size, shape, color, and taste. Likewise, if we took a random sample of genetically homogeneous tomato seeds and planted them in diverse environments, genetic material would be constant, and phenotypic trait variance would be 100% attributable to the environment ($h^2 = 0.0$). Of course, if $h^2 = 1.0$ it does not mean that the environment is irrelevant for the trait in question because genes need an environment to give them life; it only means that the environment did not contribute to the *variance* in the trait. Similarly, if $h^2 = 0.0$ it does not mean that genes did not contribute to the trait in question. It only means that genes accounted for none of the *variance* in the trait, but without genes the environment is barren. Genes provide the potential; the environment determines the extent to which that potential is actualized.

Heritability in Different Environments

Heritability coefficients are higher in advantaged than in disadvantaged environments because, like roses planted in an English garden versus the Nevada desert, advantaged environments bring out the best in the genetic material. A dramatic example of this is the average 5-inch difference in height between North and South Koreans. North and South Koreans are genetically the same people, so this gap must be attributed to their different environments. Heritability is higher among the taller South Koreans because their nutrition needs are more sufficiently met there than in North Korea, so their environment (which is more constant) is a less important component in height variation in South Korea than genes. In North Korea, access to nutritional food is far more variable, and so the environment (one's political status in the dictatorship) contributes more to height variation. Thus, the greater the environmental equality relative to the trait in question, the more genes contribute to it (Schwekendiek, 2009).

Advantaged environments offer a greater range of opportunities for individuals to choose their path in life consistent with their desires, leading to more genetically influenced behaviors, and thus greater heritability coefficients (Selita, & Kovas, 2019). Disadvantaged environments (poverty, single-parent, disorganized neighborhoods) have a strong influence on behavior, and, consequently, genetic influences will be weaker, especially for genes associated with prosocial traits. They will, however, permit the expression of genes associated with antisocial traits. An individual raised in a disadvantaged environment is analogous to planting roses in a weed patch and expecting them to thrive. Prosocial traits such as altruism, honesty, and conscience need careful cultivation to grow. Antisocial traits, such as low self-control, aggression, and negative emotionality, are like weeds—a default option that will shoot up through the cracks.

Turkheimer et al.'s (2003) finding of h^2 values for IQ of .72 in advantaged environments and .10 in disadvantaged environments is indicative of this. Likewise, a study of adolescent aggressive behavior found h^2 to be .70 for youths with low levels of familial conflict, .53 for youths with moderate familial conflict, and .28 for youths with high levels of familial conflict (Bartels & Hudziak, 2007). A Swedish study of 1,133 twin pairs aged found that the heritability of antisocial behavior was .37 in advantaged environments and not reliably greater than zero in disadvantaged environments. Shared environment was most important for boys (.69) in disadvantaged environments, but negligible (.13) for boys in advantaged environments (Tuvblad, Grann, & Lichtenstein, 2006).

Crime is clearly more prevalent in disadvantaged than advantaged environments, but heritability is greater in the latter. Different neighborhood crime rates reflect the mean effects of a variety of genetic and environmental risk factors. Although the mean level for genetically influenced risk factors for criminal behavior is low in advantaged environments, individuals in those environments who cross the criminal threshold typically have a greater genetic liability to do so precisely because the environment is crime-constraining. The relationship between genetics and criminality is less in disadvantaged environments because strong environmental influences mask genetic contributions, even though there are doubtless more individuals with a stronger genetic load for criminal behavior in those environments than in advantaged environments.

Shared and Non-Shared Environment

In addition to genetic effects, behavioral genetics apportions trait variance into shared (c^2) and non-shared (e^2) environmental components. Shared environments are everything twins have in common, such as familial SES, and neighborhood, and non-shared environments are those environments unique to individual twins, such as different friends and experiences. It has been invariably found that shared environmental effects on cognitive and personality traits in childhood disappear almost completely in adulthood, meaning that the environmental shaping of personalities is specific to individuals (e^2) rather than shared with siblings. Nielsen's (2006) longitudinal study of 1,072 American MZ and DZ twin pairs looked at verbal IQ (VIQ), grade-point average (GPA), and college plans (CPL) and partitioning the variance of all three measures into genetic, shared environment, and non-shared environment components. Heritability for these measures ranged from .536 to .67, e^2 ranged from .33 to .37, and c^2 ranged from .002 to .137. The variance explained by SES (shared environment) across all measures is not significantly different from zero, but the variance explained by genes and non-shared environment is substantial

The low to zero effects of shared environment in adulthood means that the shared environmental effects on personality and cognitive traits that made siblings somewhat similar while they shared a home fail to survive the period of common rearing. Burt and Simons jump on this to question the utility of the concept of heritability: "Indeed, the conclusion from many of these heritability studies that little—if any—of the variance in criminal behavior is due to shared environments, often interpreted to include parenting and community factors, contradicts a wealth of research conducted during the past century as well as the major theories of crime" (2014, p. 224). The research that behavioral genetics allegedly contradicts, however, has a totally different goal. It looks at purely environmental sources of mean differences in criminal offending between families and neighborhoods and says nothing about individual differences within them. Behavioral genetic studies showing low to zero effects of shared environment only mean that parental effects on personality and cognitive traits that made siblings somewhat similar while they shared a home fail to survive the period of common rearing. This is not the same as saying parents or communities have no effect on the *mean* level of these features. The weak effect of shared environments means only that they have few *similar* effects on adult siblings for behavioral, personality, and cognitive traits; it does not mean they have had *no* effect. Environmental factors can have large effects on the mean of any number of phenotypic traits without affecting trait *variance*. The stability of genetic variance means that heritability can remain stable even while the mean level of a variable is rising, falling, or staying the same.

Gene-Environment Interaction and Gene-Environment Correlation

Gene-environment interaction (G x E) and correlation (rGE) emphasize the inseparability of genes and environments for human development and behavior choices. We cannot predict a developmental or behavioral outcome from either genes or environments alone, only from both in combination. We do not need geneticists to tell us that people are differentially sensitive to identical environmental influences and will respond to their environments in different ways. This is the common-sense notion underlying G x E: "The heat that melts the butter hardens the egg" (Nettler, 1984, p. 295). Children with low self-control and low fear are genetically more vulnerable to opportunities for antisocial behavior in their environment than more self-controlled and fearful children. Extraverted and sensation-seeking individuals will be attracted to careers in the military, in firefighting, or the police, while those inclined to introversion and prudence will be attracted to less dangerous occupations.

The concept of rGE is based on the notion that people seek environments that are compatible with their genetic dispositions (genes and environments will covary positively). There are three kinds of rGE: passive, evocative, and active. Passive rGE is the correlation between a child's genotype and its environment; it is called "passive" because neither the child's genes nor its behavior is responsible for the correlation; rather, the correlation is the product of parents' genotypes (Sesardic, 2003). A child who receives parental genes conducive to high intelligence will doubtless find itself in an environment in which intellectual activities are modeled and reinforced, and the opposite is also doubtless true.

Evocative rGE refers to how other people in children's environments (parents, siblings, teachers, peers) react to them on the basis of their behavior. The behavior of others toward a child is as much (perhaps even more) a function of the child's evocative behavior as it is of the interaction style of the people who react to it. The behavioral characteristics and personality traits children present to others increase or decrease the probability of evoking certain kinds of responses from others. A disrespectful and bad-tempered child will evoke fewer positive responses from others than will a good-tempered and respectful child, regardless of a parent's or teacher's own traits and characteristics. Some children may evoke such punitive reactions from others that will exacerbate their already-antisocial personality and drive them to seek out others similarly predisposed ("birds of a feather"), further reinforcing their antisocial tendencies and choices. Evocative rGE thus magnifies differences among phenotypes.

Active rGE refers to the environments sought out by individuals compatible with their natures. That is, our genes nudge us in the direction of features of the social world that will be salient and rewarding to us, and we will seek them within the range of cultural freedoms and constraints. In active rGE, genes guide the individual's choice of environments which then loop back to shape and further reinforce expression of his or her disposition. Active rGE gains more explanatory power as individuals mature and acquire the ability to take greater control of their own lives and make choices. This coheres with consistent findings that MZ twins reared apart construct their own lives about as similarly as MZ twins reared together (Carey, 2003), and that MZ twins reared apart construct their environments considerably more similarly than DZ twins raised together (Bouchard & McGue, 2003).

The concept of rGE alerts us to the fact that people don't just find themselves in criminogenic environments by happenstance. Even children who have the misfortune to find themselves in bad neighborhoods and abusive families in which they have absolutely no part in creating have inherited trait dispositions from parents (passive rGE) that may lead them to perpetuate those criminogenic environments. These environmental effects exacerbate criminogenic tendencies, but we cannot know their unique contribution unless we are able to rule out self-selection into them. Without behavioral genetic designs, criminologists cannot disentangle the causal effects of the environment from those of individual traits leading to self-selection (Moffitt & Beckley, 2015).

The power of active rGE is evident from the observation that heritability increases for personality traits from childhood to adulthood because as twins grow up, they have more non-shared experiences, with DZ twins becoming much less similar to one another than MZ twins. Correlations between DZ pairs on many traits shrink as they gain the ability and the freedom to construct their own environments, and because DZ correlations shrink further than MZ correlations, heritability will increase. The empirical finding that heritability increases as we age reflects both the increasing ability of MZ twins to construct their environments similarly in accordance with their shared genes and at the same time the increasing freedom of DZ twins to construct their environments differently. Thus, human beings are active participants in the creation of environments that cohere with their genotypes when free to do so (Tuvblad & Baker, 2011).

Because genes affect differential *exposure* to environmental risks via active rGE and differential *susceptibility* to environmental risks via GxE, both processes always operate simultaneously and are difficult to untangle. In other words, people self-select into different environments on the basis of their genetically driven preferences when they are able, and because they self-select them, they will be more susceptible to its influence (GxE) than will those there by happenstance. In addition to furthering our understanding of the role of genes in understanding behavior, the concepts of GxE and rGE have yielded enormous benefits to our understanding of the role of the environment in shaping behavior; as Baker, Bezdjian, and Raine (2006, p. 44) put it: "the more we know about the genetics of behavior, the more important the environment appears to be."

Free Will within a Behavioral Genetics Context

I emphasize again that free will does not invoke noncausal processes, but it is to be understood in terms of well-reasoned cognitive processes that some people can better engage than others. This brings us back to Brembs' (2011) notion that free will lies on a continuum rather than being a binary something we either have or do not. These cognitive processes may not create the multiple alternatives one may choose from in life, but they do enable us to capitalize on them. There are many forking pathways in life that one may take, none of which are predetermined. The eventual path we choose to take may be consistent with our genes and our pasts, but they are not necessitated by them. All meaningful actions must have reasons (causes) that arise from our self-identities as they presently exist, but it is nonsense to claim that if our actions have reasons, they cannot be free within those parameters because our self-identities are us. These reasons certainly sway us, but ultimately we must choose how much they are allowed to do so.

If free will is defined as the ability to be free from one's genetic makeup and from the sum of one's past experiences, which together define our self-identity, free will requires us to be free of our self-identities, which is not possible. However, understanding the causal roles of genetics and environment makes individuals no less responsible for their choices. Genes or environments do not commit crimes; the constituted whole organism emerging from them does. Free will cannot be excluded from the deterministic structure of nature, but it must be included within it. Even as we argue for a genetic basis for a behavioral trait, we do not gainsay the importance of personal choice. Choices emerge when a person is in a situation with several ways to conclude it to the person's long-term benefit. The person begins a search of available opinions and makes a choice from among them. Neuroscientist T. T. Hills notes:

> the initiation of the search and the choice among alternatives—that is the basis of the self's emergent will and its genuine freedom. The bringing forth of a self-identity is the evaluation of alternatives through self-simulation. If a historical self emerges through conscious deliberation, and that deliberation involves simulation of alternative futures over which the self chooses, then a historical identity and the capacity for free choice arise in tandem. (2019, p. 6)

True, we do not choose either our genes or our familial environments, but within a behavioral genetic framework, we can locate free will/free mind in the concepts of active rGE and non-shared environment and the phenotype that emerges from them. In fact, Turkheimer (2011) has proposed that the non-shared (e^2) coefficient should be known as the free-will coefficient. Every meaningful choice we make has a chain of reasons and reasoning behind it that makes the choice comprehensible. In fact, it had better have, for if it does not, we are not among the sane. But that does not mean that the choice was completely determined by factors beyond our control. The task of behavioral genetics and allied sciences is not to reductively explain away free will (or human intentionality if one finds that phrase less metaphysical) but to explain it.

Chapter Four

Neuroscience and Determinism/Free Will

Neuro-Determinism

The latest threat to free will beliefs comes from the powerful techniques of neuroscience. Citing "recent experiments in neuroscience," physicists Stephen Hawking and Leonard Mlodinow flatly assert that "It is hard to imagine how free will can operate if our behavior is determined by physical law, so it seems that we are no more than biological machines and that free will is just an illusion" (2010, p. 32). Hawking and Mlodinow toe the hard determinist line that asserts that when we sense we are making "free" choices we are deluded by our inflated self-images and that in actuality we interact with the world as biological machines destined to behave in some preprogrammed way, either by genetic hardware or environmental software. In other words, when we believe we are making volitional choices it is simply a matter of becoming consciously aware of what the programmed brain has already decided what we should do, and we deceive ourselves when we think that our free intentions initiated those choices. This is neuro-determinism—my neurons made me do it. I wonder if Hawking really believed that his brilliant body of work was determined by his ravaged "biological machine," and not at all attributable to his own brilliance, perseverance, courage, and agency. The courage he manifested in continuing scientific research despite contracting amyotrophic lateral sclerosis (ALS)—a progressive neurodegenerative disease—at an early age evidences a very strong will.

Hawking and Mlodinow's appeal to "recent experiments in neuroscience" refers to a series of experiments showing that the brain registers decisions to make simple movements such as pressing buttons or moving a finger before subjects consciously decide to act. The most cited example is the famous 1983 experiment by Benjamin Libet and his colleagues (Libet, Wright Jr, & Gleason, 1983). These researchers had subjects perform simple physical tasks with EEG electrodes attached to their scalps while seated in front of an oscilloscope (an instrument that displays and analyzes electronic wave signals). A clock with a fast-circulating dot was created on the oscilloscope's screen. Subjects were asked to make movements such as moving a finger, flexing a wrist, or raising an arm whenever they felt the urge, and to then report the position of the dot on the screen when they became conscious of the decision to do so. Subjects' reports, coupled with oscilloscope readings, indicated that unconscious brain activity was observable as EEG signals about 500 ms before they reported conscious awareness of their urge to move. In other words, subjects' brains unconsciously initiated their actions about one-half second before they were consciously aware of their decisions. This was interpreted to mean that conscious intentions are not the cause of human actions but rather the consequences of unconscious brain processes; that is, the putative causes of our actions are actually the effects.

These findings were seized on by hard determinists to paint human beings as automatons adrift in a mindless universe, and it was declared a major problem for imbeciles who believe in spooky things like free will. Although there have been, and still are, many great scientists

(Einstein, for instance) who were/are hard determinists, there are many others who were/are not. Nobel laureate physicist Max Planck was no imbecile, and he believed fervently in free will, noting: "This question is of such urgent human interest that I think it will be well if I treat it here before I come to a close. It is the question of the freedom of the human will. Our own consciousness tells us that our wills are free. And the information which that consciousness directly gives us is the last and highest exercise of our powers of understanding" (2017, p. 101). Planck also states that it is unwarranted "to extend the tenets of scientific determinism to human conduct and thus shelve responsibility from the shoulders of the individual" (2017, p. 159).

But what are we to think of the findings of Libet and other such studies? Does it mean, as Greene and Cohen (2004, p. 1784) aver, that "free will as we ordinarily understand it is an illusion generated by our cognitive architecture?" I submit that Libet-like experiments should lead us to conclude no such thing. Levy and Bayne note that readiness potentials "underlie or constitute the neural substrate of desires or urges rather than intentions or decisions. No one should be surprised to find that desires precede conscious intentions, and finding that we have such desires does not commit us to act upon them. For all Libet has shown, it may be that another conscious act is necessary before the event associated with the readiness potential leads to action" (2004, p. 464). Furthermore, we should all realize that the experimental nature of such studies erects an artificial environment that in no way resembles any natural setting in which voluntary actions occur.

Similarly, Iain McGilchrist's take on such experiments is that "it is only a problem [for free will] if one imagines that, for me to decide something, I have to have willed it with the conscious part of my mind. Perhaps my unconscious is every bit as much 'me.' In fact, it had better be, because so little of life is conscious at all" (2009, p. 187). In other words, the subconscious areas of our minds are still us, and thus they are associated with our wills. After all, we obviously do not make conscious decisions to put one foot in front of the other when we walk, but our decision to walk from one place to another is ours nonetheless. To use such experiments to argue against free will ignores the fact that we have a mechanism designed to enable us to act without conscious deliberation called the autonomic nervous system (ANS), the seat of the "fight or flight" response. If someone throws a rock at you there is no time for conscious deliberation; you simply duck. You don't perceive the threat and chew it over in your mind before deciding that it is a good idea to duck.

Libet's readiness potential reflects subjects' awareness that they have to perform a task and are readying their brains for it, just as police officers ready their brains for rock throwers when responding to a riot. Likewise, Libet's observations reflect subjects' anticipation of the experimental response rather than the actual conscious implementation of the movement. That is, subjects' decision processes may be configured by their conscious intentions that they formed at the time they received the experimental task instructions. Writing about the neurophysiology of the readiness potential, Nestor (2019, p. 3) points out: "This brain wave represents slow-acting, low-frequency electrical oscillations, which more likely reflect neural mechanisms of anticipation, preparing, and planning of a response rather than the actual implementation of a movement." Recall that Libet's subjects were asked to report when they felt an "urge" to move. An urge may initiate a decision, but it is not a decision.

The point is that no one consciously initiates mundane actions. I may, for instance, consciously decide to drive to the mall to look around, but I would not ruminate about finishing my coffee, reaching for my car keys, walking to the car, or on how to brake for darting pedestrians along the way. All these mundane things are not consciously initiated; I leave them to the good graces of my central (my brain) and peripheral (my ANS) nervous systems. This does not mean that my conscious consideration to visit the mall did not initiate these "downstream" reflexive actions. If someone wants to say that my decision to go to the mall determined those actions, that's fine, but I defy anyone who tells me that at the moment of my conscious decision to visit the mall with no particular goal in mind that I was compelled to do so and could not have done otherwise. One could concoct a deterministic argument and say that I was bored or my wife was nagging me to mow the lawn and I wished to escape either of these negative conditions, or perhaps I had an innate "shopping disposition," but such a concoction would be a caricature of determinism by turning soft *reasons* into hard *causes*. Furthermore, conscious intentions are causally efficacious, so it was my conscious intention that set me on the way to the mall, and that's free mind.

In other experiments, Libet instructed subjects to stop their intended actions once they became aware of the urge to carry them out. Subjects had a window of about 150 milliseconds after the subconscious urge to complete the task in which to consciously veto the urge. Libet notes:

> Subjects can in fact "veto" motor performance during a 100-200-ms period before a prearranged time to act. The role of conscious will would be not to initiate a specific voluntary act but rather to select and control volitional outcome. It is proposed that conscious will can function in a permissive fashion, either to permit or to prevent the motor implementation of the intention to act that arises unconsciously. (1985, p. 529)

He called this abortive process "free won't." We exercise free won't every time we abort an automatic subconscious urge to light that cigarette, take another beer, or to initiate an illicit relationship because it is the process of exercising self-control over our immediate desires (or what Schopenhauer called our wills).

To interpret Libet's findings to mean that we are automatons ignores the fact that when decisions of importance are made in everyday life they are never as simple as "When will I move my finger or flex my wrist." You don't automatically act when deciding things that have a major impact on your life such as asking your girlfriend to marry you, buying a house, quitting a job, or where to go on vacation. These decisions require conscious thought, including thoughts relating to the constraints that hamper your decision. Conscious thought enables you to mentally simulate alternative possibilities of action and the possible consequences of each alternative. This is what free will is; desiring (willing) something and then consciously and rationally deciding if that's really what you should do and how you should go about doing it.

It is important to note that Libet did not interpret his results, or similar results obtained by others, the way Hawkins and many others did. On the contrary, Libet was a firm believer in free will and says as much:

> My conclusion about free will, one genuinely free in the non-determined sense, is then that its existence is at least as good, if not a better, scientific option than is its denial by determinist theory. ... Such a view would at least allow us to proceed in a way that accepts and accommodates our own deep feeling that we do have free will. We would not need to view ourselves as machines that act in a manner completely controlled by the known physical laws. (Libet, 1999, pp. 56–57)

Ironically, the man most often credited as the destroyer of free will was a firm believer in it. So, what would a person be like if he or she really believed that free will is an illusion; I mean a person who was convinced of it, not just one parroting the words of famous free will deniers such as Hawking or neuroscientist Sam Harris? I submit that such people claiming that they can do nothing to alter the course of their lives would quickly descend into a dark sinkhole of unhappiness, despair, alienation, and victimhood. The intuition that we are the masters of our own fate is imperative if we are to live meaningful lives.

A number of psychological experiments have shown that people who dismiss the idea of free will grant themselves the right to behave immorally. Experiments involving college students found that students exposed to positive messages of determinism were significantly more likely to cheat on a variety of tasks than students exposed to positive messages of free will. The authors of one such study concluded that "Much as thoughts of death and meaninglessness can induce existential angst that can lead to ignoble behaviors, doubting one's free will may undermine the sense of self as agent. Or, perhaps, denying free will simply provides the ultimate excuse to behave as one likes" (Vohs & Schooler, 2008, p. 54). Criminologists have long identified the fatalistic belief that one is the slave of outside influences as one of the features of people occupying the lowest rungs of society and that it is a belief that spawns hostility toward mainstream culture and promotes criminal behavior. Such people feed on the notion that powerful others have somehow arranged society in such a way as to keep them down and thus there is nothing they can do about it.

The Compatibilist Option

The free will/determinism debate is seen by many as cast in only dichotomous terms, much like the nature/nurture debate in psychology or the capitalism/socialism debate in economics used to be. No one talks of nature *or* nurture anymore, but rather in terms of nature *via* nurture. The capitalist/socialist dichotomy has likewise dissolved in a continuum as we recognize that all wealthy free-market countries have a large helping of socialist-type welfare programs. We can adopt a similar position on the free will/determinism debate in the philosophical position called compatibilism. Just as few scholars today hold dichotomous positions on the nature/nurture or capitalist/socialism issues, Pockett (2007, p. 282) tells us: "Many, or even most, present-day philosophers are so-called compatibilists." Compatibilism is a "middle-ground" position that insists that free will and determinism can peacefully coexist because one can accept both without being logically inconsistent.

Both free will and determinism are representations of human reality, and we all interpret to conduct of self and others in compatibilist terms. We ascribe conscious intentions to free will but explain motives and behavior by assuming that they are the products of genetics and developmental experiences. Explanations, however, are *ex post facto* reasons for behavior; they are not excuses that imply that the behavior in question was compelled. Compatibilism acknowledges that while humans are never free of involuntary dispositions or external influences, human actions are free within that causal space because those dispositions are ours and external influences are just that—influences leaning us toward one choice rather than another without necessitating it. This soft determinism does not deny that human events have a chain of prior events leading to them but avers that as long as we are free from external coercion, we have the freedom to decide how to respond to those events in positive or negative ways. We can ask how free a person is in circumstance X, or how determined a person is in circumstance Y. The criminal justice systems of all civilized societies are compatibilist in that they hold criminals responsible for their actions yet leave space for a variety of mitigating factors (mental disease or defect, coercion, etc.) that remove them from the purview of complete responsibility when sentencing them for their crimes.

Adherents of both libertarian free will and hard determinism view their respective positions as logically incompatible and thus see compatibilism as evading the issue, but compatibilists may counter this objection by analogizing compatibilism with Nobel laureate physicist Niels Bohr's principle of complementarity—the wave/particle dual nature of light. There was much initial resistance among physicists to this counterintuitive duality since they reasoned that natural phenomena cannot be two things at the same time, but Bohr saw this apparent paradox as an opportunity rather than a stumbling block: "How wonderful that we have met with a paradox. Now we have some hope of making progress" (in Sharma et al., 2013, p. 107). As this complementarity became more and more empirically endorsed, it led to modern quantum theory. Albert Einstein and Leopold Infeld had the following to say about this supposed conundrum:

> But what is light really? Is it a wave or a shower of photons? There seems no likelihood for forming a consistent description of the phenomena of light by a choice of only one of the two languages. It seems as though we must use sometimes the one theory and sometimes the other, while at times we may use either. We are faced with a new kind of difficulty. We have two contradictory pictures of reality; separately neither of them fully explains the phenomena of light, but together they do. (1938, pp. 262–263)

Compatibilists maintain that human beings exhibit this same complementary duality and may likewise ask: "But what is human action really?" Substitute human action for light, free will and determinism for waves and particles, and we can also conclude that neither free will nor determinism alone can explain human behavior; we need both concepts to do so. After all, we all interpret the conduct of ourselves and others through both these frames of reference. We ascribe conscious motives to our free will, and at the same time assume soft determinism when explaining behavior as the product of various past or present circumstances. That is, although voluntary actions and inclinations may be initiated by one's free will, they nevertheless proceed from a complex web of influences that one may not be fully, or not at all, consciously aware of. We cannot engage our free minds without simultaneously engaging those externalities. Just as there is no longer any paradox in the wave/particle duality of light, there should be no paradox in viewing humans as both free agents and determined since freedom and determinism are inextricably intertwined. While our dispositions may not be subject to our voluntary control, and neither are the environments and situations we find ourselves in, our actions within them can be. This kind of soft determinism—a kind of psychological "uncertainty principle"—gives us the only kind of free will worth having. It is a free will/free mind that allows us to follow the rationally reasoned appetitive dictates of our nature and to eschew its aversions, but it also lays on our shoulders the responsibility of owning our actions.

Niels Bohr himself was quite comfortable with complementarity, or compatibilism, in human affairs. Bohr noted that the interaction of human beings with their environments precludes viewing them as fully determined systems mechanistically responding to stimuli in foreordained fashion. He saw the complementarity of free will and determinism as existing in the purposeful actions of the free subjective self on the one hand, and the deterministic objective self, with all its dispositions and formative experiences, as subject to causality, on the other. He reasoned that whatever these dispositions of experiences may be, the subjective self has the power to transcend them and decide whether or not to initiate an action in response to them. In his approach to the explanation of actions, he notes that if we are to have a "harmonious" life we must accept this complementarity: "Altogether, the approach towards the problem of explanation that is embodied in the notion of complementarity suggests itself in our position as conscious beings and recalls forcefully the teaching of ancient thinkers that, in the search for a harmonious attitude towards life, it must never be forgotten that we ourselves are both actors and spectators in the drama of existence" (1950, p. 54).

As a compatibilist, I realize that everything I am is the result of my genome and my developmental experiences that I did not will into existence and for which I can claim neither pride nor shame. But now that I have this particular character and personality that inclines me to behave in one way or another, I alone must decide how I should act. I have illicit feelings and desires that intrude on me from time to time which I can act upon, or like Jimmy Carter's thoughts of adultery, I can set aside. I am not morally responsible for those feelings and desires, for as Schopenhauer reminded us, we cannot will (control) what we desire. However, I have free mind to decide what I shall do, and am thus morally responsible for whatever action my decision initiated.

Neuroscience and the Juvenile Death Penalty

Neuroscience has had a big impact on the U.S. legal system, particularly in its role in getting rid of the death penalty for those whose crimes were committed before age 18. To obtain a conviction, the law is required to prove a guilty act (*actus reus*) and guilty intent *(mens rea).* The latter asks if a defendant rationally knew that harm would result from one's actions. Guilty intent implies free-willed action, but neuroscience raises the issue of how much of this we can ascribe to youthful vis-a-vis adult offenders. It has challenged the idea that juveniles can form guilty intent by focusing on the emotional irrationality of much of youthful conduct. The New York Academy of Sciences 2003 conference on adolescent brain development (White, 2004) noted that there is a lack of synchrony between a physically mature body and a still maturing nervous system in adolescents, and they have a more reward-sensitive brain relative to children and adults. These undoubtedly true observations had a major impact on the U.S. Supreme Court's ruling in *Roper v. Simmons* (2005).

In 1993, 17-year-old Christopher Simmons and two younger accomplices burglarized the home of Shirley Crook, kidnapped her, tied her, beat her, and threw her alive off a bridge into the river below to drown. There was never any doubt that Simmons was guilty, and he never claimed otherwise. Simmons had told friends before the crime that he wanted to commit murder and bragged about having done so afterward. Thus, his premeditated offense clearly involved the requisite guilty intent. Simmons was sentenced to death for this brutal crime. The issue before the Court in *Roper* was how much blameworthiness we can ascribe to young offenders relative to adults. The Court said it was less, and ruled the death penalty for juvenile offenders to be unconstitutional (Hatch & Walsh, 2016).

I concur with the Court's ruling, and the findings of neuroscience about the immaturity of the juvenile brain have been replicated in many hundreds of fMRI and PET scan studies, but does that mean that juveniles lack free will, or just have less of it? Juveniles can't be expected to rationally weigh the consequences of their decisions the way most adults can, nor can they delay gratification in the same way because their reasoning process is freighted with too much emotion. This is a mitigating factor, but not an excusatory one, and not one that takes free will, albeit more limited than adult free will, from juveniles. The compatibilist adult legal system places less culpability (less free will) on "heat of passion" murders and on murderers with IQs below 70 (another brain-based factor) and views them as mitigating factors.

However, neuroscience relies only on probabilistic generalizations about adolescents as a *class of individuals* from numerous brain scans average across all studies; it is not very helpful in making highly individualized determinations about *specific* juveniles before the court. As Jones and Shen put it: "Just because a particular pattern of neural activity, on average at the group level, with impaired decision-making, it does not necessarily follow that the defendant before the court whose brain scans produce the same neural patterns necessarily has a cognitive defect" (2012, p. 356). Making inferences about specific individuals and their intentions from aggregate data derived from the group to which he or she belongs is to commit the ecological fallacy.

We may ask if Christopher Simmons' 17-year-old brain was any less mature than millions of other adolescents who did not plan, execute, and brag about a horrendous crime. His planned actions were fully indicative of his ability to form the requisite *mens rea,* and hardly indicative of impulsiveness or that his brutal actions were beyond his control. Even if crimes are committed impulsively, "crimes committed impulsively ... are still committed consciously and intentionally" (Morse, 2006, p. 406). To argue that Simmons' crime was a direct result of the normal adolescent maturational process that we all experienced is fallacious. Adolescence can be a trying time, but the overwhelming majority of us emerge from it without committing horrible crimes. If we are to abolish the death penalty for all, it should be based on humanistic ethics and not at the expense of that which makes us human—our free minds.

As with the rest of us, Simmons has a brain that evolved to fit him into a civilized culture that requires him to self-regulate, to intentionally inhibit antisocial impulse, and to act civilized. He had the necessary neurological equipment to enable him to do that, and a culture full of "Thou shalts" and "shalt nots" to guide him. As Roy Baumeister states, only if he lacked these things could he be said to lack the free will to do otherwise:

> The capacity for free action was created by evolution, most likely the specific requirements of evolution for functioning in culture. Self-control, rational choice, and ad hoc planning reflect the operation of this new sort of processes, which appears to depend on transforming the body's energy (carried in the blood as glucose) into advanced psychological operations. Free will depends on conscious, meaningful thought, which again invokes the connection to culture and suggests that anatomically intact human animals who grew up without culture would lack free will. (2014, p. 235)

Chapter Five

Free Will, Locus of Control, Personality, and Criminality

Free Will, Locus of Control, and Political Ideology

A major psychological concept associated with the free will concept is locus of control. The locus of control idea posits that individuals differ in the extent to which they either believe that they control the course of their lives or that external factors determine them. "An internal locus of control reflects the perception that reinforcements are principally caused by an individual's behavior or characteristics. In contrast, an external locus of control reflects the perception that reinforcements are triggered by factors external to the individual, such as chance, fate or other people" (Farnier et al., 2021, p. 3514). Individuals with a deterministic worldview tend to have an external locus of control, and those with a free will worldview tend to have an internal locus of control (Hannikainen et al., 2017).

Of course, few people act with the belief that they alone completely determine everything that happens in their lives, and few believe or act as though they have no control over what happens to them. However, in many respects, individuals' locus of control perspective reflects their perception of their capacity for agency—the extent to which they feel they are capable of engaging with the world to meet their needs and goals, and their capacity for agency has much to do with the extent to which they harbor free will beliefs (Heffernan & Ward, 2017). When criminologists study criminals, they do so with unstated assumptions about criminals' locus of control, and this highlights the division among liberal and conservative scholars in how they view so many issues in criminology and criminal justice. As evidenced in their favored theories of criminality, conservative criminologists tend to have a more positive view of personal agency and thus attribute an internal locus of control to criminals and are therefore more apt to hold them responsible for their behavior. Liberal criminologists tend to attribute an external locus of control to criminals and are thus more apt to search for causes external to them for their behavior (Cooper, Walsh, & Ellis, 2010; Tyler, Heffernan, & Fortune, 2020).

These two loci of control and the ideological liberal/conservative divide on the issue are showcased in a nationwide poll about factors relating to wealth and poverty. This poll found that self-declared strong liberals believe the top reasons for people's level of wealth are factors external to individuals such as family connections (48%), inheritance (40%), and getting lucky (31%). Strong conservatives maintained that the top reasons are personality characteristics such as hard work (62%), ambition (47%), and self-discipline (45%). As for the causes of poverty, strong liberals say the top causes are discrimination (51%), an unfair economic system (48%), and lack of educational opportunities (48%), while strong conservatives say that the problems are poor life choices (60%), lack of work ethic (52%), breakdown of families (47%), and abuse of drugs and alcohol (47%) (Ekins, 2019).

Of course, these attributions of loci of control reflect differing *general* views of liberals and conservatives relative to the internal or external contributions to wealth and poverty that are not applicable across the board. Economic (and other) outcomes reflect a complicated mixture of both internal dispositions and external circumstances. Even the most self-controlled and conscientious person may sink into poverty due to unfortunate circumstances beyond the person's control, such as an economic recession and job loss, or a devastating illness, and some wealthy individuals may be wealthy even though they lack self-control and conscientiousness because of family connections or luck. On the other hand, some people are doubtless poor despite the opportunities they may have had because they lack the personal characteristics that would have enabled them to grasp those opportunities. The divide between liberals and conservatives is primarily where they place the emphasis. We should also be aware that, like the free will/determinism issue, beliefs about the loci of control are not dichotomous; they lie on a continuum and can fluctuate from time to time and with the issue at hand. This is reflected in the Ekins (2019) poll showing that only a slight majority of conservatives (52%) agreed with the question: "my life is determined by my own actions"; 33% of liberals also agreed with the statement. The 19 percentage-point difference is not that large when it comes to questions of one own's life.

The Serenity Prayer attributed to Reinhold Niebuhr provides excellent guidance for understanding the balance between the things we cannot control and the things that we can:

> God, give me grace to accept with serenity
> the things that cannot be changed,
> Courage to change the things
> which should be changed,
> and the Wisdom to distinguish
> the one from the other.

Wisdom allows people to know when to accept what they plainly cannot control and when to practice courage by accepting responsibility for things that they plainly can. There is little in this life we can actually control, but we can control ourselves and how we respond to what it throws our way. Alcoholics Anonymous enthusiastically embraces the Serenity Prayer as providing the balance between accepting the fact that one is an alcoholic and the courage to take responsibility for maintaining sobriety. Avoiding responsibility for one's life may provide some short-term relief but it carries with it a long-term cost, for falling into victimhood, as many criminals do, only serves to make the problems they face more intractable. Maintaining sobriety "one day at a time" is a lot more difficult for the alcoholic than maintaining lawful behavior on a daily basis is for the criminal. Alcoholics have a *physiological* craving for alcohol; a criminal has no such desperate craving for crime.

There is a large literature on the locus of control affirming a liberal/conservative average difference in the construct. One study noted: "The results indicate supporters for the two major parties are wired differently, in line with previous findings about ideology. Democrats were driven by an external locus of control and Republicans by an internal locus" (Sweetser, 2014, p. 1183). Another study linked locus of control to motivation and belief in free will: "Evidence from three studies reveals a critical difference in self-control as a function of political ideology. Specifically, greater endorsement of political conservatism was associated with greater attention regulation and task persistence … this relationship is shown to stem from varying beliefs in freewill [conservative belief stronger]" (Clarkson et al., 2015, p. 8250). Self-control and task persistence (conscientiousness) are traits in short supply among criminals.

In terms of the relationship between free will beliefs and locus of control, among a sample of college students Paulhus and Carey (2011) found that an internal locus of control was significantly related to belief in free will (r = .35) and negatively related to "fatalistic" (as opposed to "scientific") determinism (r = − .19). Those who endorsed an external locus of control, defined as one's life as being under the control of "powerful others," showed a non-significant negative correlation with free will but there was a significant positive relationship with (r = .29) to fatalistic determinism. It is no accident that another study found that students with strong belief in free will reported greater expectations of future occupational success (Stillman, Baumeister, & Mele, 2011). And in a field study conducted among day laborers, Stillman et al. (2010) found that those with a strong belief in free will had an internal locus of control, and performed better at work (consistently showing up for work on time, putting more effort into their work, and having a positive influence on other workers).

Because an internal locus of control is related to free will beliefs, disengaging from those beliefs to come to believe that factors other than one's self controls one's life can lead to negative consequences. Rigoni et al. (2012) found that undermining free will beliefs degrades self-control and that disbelieving in free will leads to antisocial tendencies:

> Perceived self-control is crucial for feeling responsible and accountable for one's own actions: we feel more responsible for an action that we intentionally executed than for an action that was performed involuntarily (e.g. a reflexive movement). One possible explanation of the increased antisocial tendencies after exposure to anti-free will messages might be that belief manipulation undermines personal responsibility and accountability. Feelings of responsibility and accountability promote socially desirable actions, such as altruism and impulse control, and thus undermining free will could act as a catalyst for impulsive behavior ("I could not do otherwise!"). (p. 1483)

Free Will, Locus of Control, and Life Satisfaction

Free will beliefs are associated with many facets of a person's complex amalgam of attitudes, beliefs, personality, and outlook on life that have significance for understanding criminal behavior. Belief in free will is consistently found to be a key component of positive psychology and trait happiness (Seligman, 2002). As Csikszentmihalyi and Wong (2014, p. 197) note: "happy individuals also score high on measures of internality, i.e., a tendency to attribute outcomes to oneself rather than to external causes. Happy people perceive a high degree of control and tend to believe that they have choice in their activities." Belief in free will has been shown to correlate positively with life satisfaction, happiness, and self-control: "Belief in free will has correlated positively with life satisfaction and finding life meaningful, with self-efficacy and self-control, with low levels of stress, and (though not entirely consistently) with internal locus of control" (Baumeister & Brewer, 2012, p. 736). And Farnier et al. (2021, p. 3515) found that the locus of control was associated with mental health differences: "the internal locus of control was positively related to positive mental health indicators while the external dimensions showed the opposite pattern." The belief that the negative outcomes that occur in one's life are beyond one's control can easily lead to alienation from the putative "cause" (such as an "unfair society") and a depressive and cynical outlook on life. On the other hand, an internal locus of control orientation acts as a buffer against the effects of negative life events on psychological well-being.

Indeed, Twenge, Zhang, and Im (2004, p. 315) have linked external locus of control with cynicism and alienation: "Greater cynicism and alienation leads people to believe that their personal actions mean little. Blaming others for negative events has also become more popular, and people are less likely to believe that anyone can be a success despite obstacles in the way." Crescioni et al. (2016) found that the belief in free will was positively correlated with global subjective happiness ($r = .56$) and life satisfaction ($r = .59$), and in two large Chinese cohorts, Li et al. (2017) showed that belief in free will was significantly positively related to measures of life satisfaction, positive affect, openness to experience, conscientiousness, extraversion, and agreeableness, and significantly negatively correlated with negative affect and neuroticism. These positive and negative relationships define prosocial and antisocial individuals, respectively (Gierowski & Rajtar, 2003; Miller & Lynam, 2001).

Locus of Control, Happiness, and Genetics

Measures of happiness are rarely found in the criminological literature, but we have seen that happiness is strongly related to locus of control and that an internal locus of control (and belief in free will) is negatively related to criminal offending. Comparing the personality traits of 100 Indian criminals and 100 non-criminals of similar SES background, Singh and Rani (2017, p. 66) found that unhappiness most strongly distinguished the two groups: "The unhappiness, anxiety, inferiority, risk taking, irresponsibility, assertiveness and impulsiveness are the personality traits which discriminate criminals from the non-criminals." If locus of control is associated quite strongly with life satisfaction/happiness, what is the direction of causation? It could be either way, or it could be that each has mutually reinforcing effects on the other. Environmental circumstances account almost exclusively for variance in situational happiness, but there is a genetic baseline for evaluative (subjective) happiness which moves up or down depending on circumstance, but which returns to the genetic set-point as memories of the circumstance (either good or bad) fade (Nes et al., 2006). Nes and Røysamb posit that a genetic set-point that shifts back and forth but returns to homeostasis makes sense from an evolutionary perspective because life is full of unpredictable events that necessitate flexible responses:

> Those of our ancestors whose emotional experiences mapped more accurately to their situation clearly had a selective advantage. A baseline level of emotional functioning constitutes an important prerequisite for noticing and detecting important situational changes (e.g., threats, opportunities) required for such fitting responses to external demands. Lower fitness should therefore be associated with too rapid mood swings to the extremes as well as with entirely stable moods. In accordance with these expectations, recent experimental research indicates that too much positive as well as too much negative emotion variability is often maladaptive, signaling psychological instability and psychopathology inconsistent with the concept of evolutionary fitness. Positive emotion thus seems to serve an adaptive function if it stays relatively stable over time. (2017, p. 1542)

There are a number of situational factors (e.g., good marriage, good income, many friends) that contribute to people's happiness, but if happiness has a genetic set-point, one that is set high will make a person attractive to potential spouses, bosses, and friends, and the opposite will be true for those with a low set-point. A number of meta-analyses report heritability estimates for subjective well-being and life satisfaction of between .32 and .40 (Nes & Røysamb, 2017) depending on population, context, and how those evaluations are measured. Given that happiness has a genetic set-point, one might assume that happiness levels lead one to adopt a particular locus of control but it may be that locus of control and life satisfaction/happiness have feedback effects that are mutually reinforcing.

Using a representative sample of 973 twin pairs, Weiss, Bates, and Luciano (2008) found that heritable differences in subjective well-being may be accounted for by a common genetic structure associated with the Big Five personality traits. They found that "the genetic correlations (rg) between subjective well-being and Neuroticism, Extraversion, Openness, Agreeableness, and Conscientiousness were equal to .58, .66, .21, .20, and .32, respectively" (2008, p. 208). All correlations have a positive sign because they are r's between genetics and traits, not between traits and happiness. Low neuroticism (or high emotional stability) and high extraversion were strongly related to subjective well-being, high conscientiousness less so, and openness and agreeableness weakly so. The authors conclude: "These findings indicate that subjective well-being is linked to personality by common genes and that personality may form an 'affective reserve' relevant to set-point maintenance and changes in set point over time" (2008, p. 205).

The genetic correlations in the above Weiss, Bates, and Luciano (2008) study are not the same as heritability coefficients. A genetic correlation is the proportion of variance shared by different traits due to the overlap between the two sets of genetic influences. A rg of 0.0 implies that the genetic effects on the traits in question are independent of each other; a rg of 1.0 implies that all the genetic influences on the traits are identical. Thus, 58% of the genetic influence on neuroticism is identical to the genetic influence on happiness. Had neuroticism been couched in terms of its opposite—emotional stability—the genetic correlation would be negative indicating that as the genetic influences on neuroticism increase, the genetic influences on happiness decrease. Alternatively, as the genetic influences on emotional stability increase, the genetic influences on happiness increase (Tielbeek et al., 2018).

Locus of Control-Related Personality Traits and Criminality

Before looking at the locus of control and other personality traits and criminality, it should be noted that criminologists of different political ideologies view the locus of control among criminals differently. In Cooper, Walsh, and Ellis' (2010) survey of criminologists who attended to 2007 American Society of Criminology conference, criminologists were asked their political orientation (conservative, moderate, liberal, or radical) and to rank what they considered the most important causes of crime. Consistent with locus of control differences, conservatives and moderates favored individual explanations most strongly, and liberals and radicals favored external explanations most strongly. The top three factors for conservatives were "Lack of empathy and concern for others," "Impulsiveness and risk-taking tendencies," and "Unstable family life." The top three favored by moderates were "Lack of empathy and concern for others," "Poor discipline practices," and "Unstable family life." The top three liberal factors were "Unfair economic system," "Lack of educational opportunities," and "Peer influences." For radicals, the top three were "Unfair economic system," "Bias in law enforcement," and "Lack of educational opportunities." It is clear that conservatives (and moderates) lean toward an internal locus of control, and that liberals and radicals lean toward an external locus of control, with radicals appearing to attribute criminal behavior to external factors even more than liberals. It must be stressed again that the disagreement is where the emphasis is placed rather than a complete denial of the putative causes favored by their ideological counterparts.

All of these alleged causes doubtlessly have an impact on a person's decision to engage in criminal offending, particularly so if offenders perceive these external factors to be true. We will not have an inkling of which are the most powerful causes until we have a decade or so of robust studies that directly pit environmental causes against personal causes, but that is not important for our present purposes emphasizing the role of free will, agency, and the locus of control in criminal behavior. A review focusing on the locus of control by Tyler, Heffernan, and Fortune (2020) noted the importance of the locus of control to offending:

> Individuals who have offended tend to report having a more externally oriented locus of control than non-offending individuals, with this finding replicated across both adult and adolescent samples and a range of behaviors, including sexual offending, drunk driving, parents "at risk" of child abuse, and shoplifting. Further, within offending populations, individuals who have been involved in interpersonal violence (e.g., violence, sexual offending) have been found to have a more externalized locus of control compared to non-violent offending controls. Individuals with an external locus of control are also reported to be more likely to reoffend than those with an internal locus of control. (p. 2; internal references omitted)

As for personality traits associated with locus of control and criminality, among a sample of incarcerated Polish criminals, Gierowski and Rajtar (2003) found that neuroticism ($r = .34$) and psychoticism ($r = .53$) correlated positively with an external locus of control, and a negative correlation between external locus of control and the general indicator of a person's sense of coherence ($r = -.45$). Thus, the higher the general level of coherence the prisoner had, the lower his belief in external locus of control. The principle of coherence encompasses *comprehensibility* (the belief that internal and external stimuli are structured, explainable, and controllable by the person), *meaningfulness* (the belief that one has the resources to cope with these stimuli in meaningful ways), and *manageability* (the person views demand stimuli as challenges worthy of effort and commitment). Similarly, Dahiru and Oshishepo's (2019) Nigerian prison inmates study found that an external locus of control significantly influences criminal behavior. Of the inmates who scored above the mean on criminal behavior, 54.3% had an external locus of control and 10% had an internal locus of control. Even among non-criminals, Tsai, Wang, and Lo (2014) found that among Taiwanese athletes the higher the level of belief in external locus of control, the more their moral disengagement in sports and the more frequent their rule violations.

Conscientiousness, Agreeableness, and Criminality

Since conscientiousness and agreeableness have both been shown to be related to free will beliefs and locus of control, I will concentrate only on these two constructs in the final section of this chapter. Conscientiousness is a primary trait composed of several sub-traits such as well-organized, disciplined, scrupulous, responsible, and reliable at one pole, and disorganized, careless, unreliable, irresponsible, and unscrupulous at the other. It is easy to see how low conscientiousness could be directly related to crime through the inability of people who lack it to follow a legitimate path to the American Dream: "It is not merely a matter of talented individuals confronted with inferior schools and discriminatory hiring practices. Rather, a good deal of research indicates that many delinquents and criminals are untalented individuals who cannot compete effectively in complex industrial societies" (Vold, Bernard, & Snipes, 1998, p. 177). In other words, persons with low conscientiousness do not have the personal qualities needed to apply themselves to the long and arduous task of achieving financial success legitimately, and as a consequence may attempt to obtain it illegitimately.

Agreeableness is the tendency to be friendly, considerate, courteous, helpful, and cooperative with others. Agreeable persons tend to trust others, compromise with them, empathize with and aid them. This list of sub-traits suggests a high degree of concern for prosocial conformity and social desirability. Disagreeable persons simply display the opposite characteristics—suspicion of others, unfriendly, uncooperative, unhelpful, and lacking empathy—which all suggest a lack of concern for prosocial conformity and social desirability. While agreeable people tend to also be conscientious, this is not always the case. A person can be very conscientious at work but thoroughly disagreeable as a person (think of the greedy, egotistical, and manipulative corporate criminal), and one can be very agreeable but be lackadaisical at work (think of the ritualist of Robert Merton's anomie theory).

Agreeableness appears to be a better protective factor against criminality than conscientiousness. In Miller and Lynam's (2001) meta-analysis comparing prisoner with non-prisoner samples, they found moderate to strong negative relationships between agreeableness and antisocial behavior and moderate negative relationships between conscientiousness and antisocial behavior. Miller and Lynam (2001, p. 780) describe the personality of the "typical" criminal in terms of agreeableness and conscientiousness: "Individuals who commit crimes tend to be hostile, self-centered, spiteful, jealous, and indifferent to others (i.e., low in Agreeableness). They tend to lack ambition, motivation, and perseverance, have difficulty controlling their impulses and hold nontraditional and unconventional values and beliefs (i.e., are low in Conscientiousness)."

Chapter Six

Free Will in the Classical and Positivist Schools

Cesare Beccaria and the Despotic Spirit

Modern Criminology is the product of two main schools of thought that arose in Italy: the classical school originating in the 18th century and the positivist school originating in the 19th century. The classical school championed free will, the positive school championed determinism, and various theoretical versions of both schools have butted heads ever since. Nye (1976) characterized this deep division:

> Although elsewhere in Europe the lines between free will and determinism in criminality were by no means drawn as sharply as in Italy, by 1885 there had emerged two distinct doctrinal alternatives. On one side were the free-will "metaphysicians," who were largely jurists and penal authorities, and on the other were those for whom criminal anthropology provided the unifying focus-doctors of psychiatry, neurologists, and doctors of legal medicine. Opinions were sometimes mediated on a practical level, but theoretically nearly all observers believed it necessary to choose one or the other position. (1976, p. 337)

The father of classical criminology is the Italian nobleman and professor of law, Cesare Bonesana, Marchese di Beccaria. In 1764, Beccaria published a work calling for the reform of judicial and penal systems throughout Europe, *On Crimes and Punishment* (1963). The book was written in reaction to the savage laws and barbaric punishments that existed in Europe at the time. It is a passionate plea to reform the criminal justice system, humanize and rationalize the law, and make punishment more just and humane. Prior to Beccaria, the law was a severely cruel "law and order" system of social control aimed at the protection of the privileged few from the predations of the "inferior" classes.

Beccaria's philosophy was informed by Enlightenment ideas of the dignity of the human person. He emphasized the popular "social contract" notions of Hobbes and Locke that citizens give up certain rights in order to gain security and protection from the state. Although within this idea is the assumption that laws are supposed to be just compacts between citizens and the state aimed at the peace and security of all, they were marked by judicial arbitrariness, bias, and barbaric penalties. Beccaria championed the idea that justice demands that equals be treated equally and unequals treated unequally according to relevant differences. By "equal" and "unequal" he was referring to the equality of severity of the crimes offenders commit. That is, punishment must be matched with the severity of the crime. This matching was the only relevant difference to be considered for the purpose of deciding criminals' punishment, not their social status or any other aspect of their lives. We see Beccaria's notion instantiated in modern sentencing guidelines that refer to crime seriousness and prior record as the only determinants of punishment severity for convicted criminals.

Beccaria's work focused on penal and judicial and made no effort to plumb the depths of criminal character or motivation, arguing that crime is simply the result of "the despotic spirit which is in every man" (1963, p. 12). Beccaria was thus asserting that everyone was equally capable of committing crimes and that there were no real differences between criminals and non-criminals except that the former had freely made conscious choices to violate the law. Non-criminals were people who overcame the human passion for depravity and who freely choose to live within the law. Beccaria thus saw both criminals and non-criminals as active volitional decision-makers. He argued that the temptation to surrender to the "despotic spirit" must be countered by the threat of punishment, which had to be certain, swift, and severe enough to outweigh any benefits offenders may get from their crimes if they are to be deterred from future crimes. He elaborated on these three elements of punishment as follows:

Certainty: "[t]he certainty of punishment, even if it be moderate, will always make a stronger impression that the fear of another which is more terrible but combined with the hope of impunity" (1963, p. 58).

Swiftness: "[t]he more promptly and the more closely punishment follows upon the commission of a crime, the more just and useful will it be" (1963, p. 55).

Severity: "For a punishment to attain its end, the evil which it inflicts has only to exceed the advantage derivable from the crime; in this excess of evil one should include the … loss of the good which the crime might have produced. All beyond this is superfluous and for that reason tyrannical" (1963, p. 43).

Many criminologists find this to be an overly simplistic deterrence theory freighted with faulty assumptions about human nature and free will, but others find it more than adequate to account for variation in crime rates across time within various political entities. For instance, Michael Gottfredson notes: "To many, the logic of the theory is compelling. All people calculate advantages and all people fear punishments (or at least can be made to fear them). The personal gains from crime are, to most people, obvious. Thus, if crime rates are too high, or are increasing, modification of state penalties must be in order" (2011, p. 131). Beccaria made no room for individual differences in the ability to calculate in response to punitive sanctions or how various positive and negative factors are weighted for this was not his intention, but Gottfredson and Hirschi's self-control concept can be of use here. Feldman (2017, p. 8) remarks: "There are conceptual links between belief in free will and self-control. Self-control allows the person to overcome some internal constraints that limit free will, such as urges, needs, temptations, and desires, and therefore some argue that self-control, together with the capacity for rational choice, are two adaptive forms of expressing free will."

Jeremy Bentham and Human Nature

Another prominent figure of the classical school was the British lawyer and philosopher Jeremy Bentham, who was deeply influenced by Beccaria's work. Bentham's major work, *Principles of Morals and Legislation* (1948), first published in 1789, is essentially a philosophy of social control based on the principle of utility, which prescribes "the greatest happiness for the greatest number." The principle of utility posits that any human action should be judged moral or immoral by its effect on the happiness of the entire community. Thus, the proper function of the legislature is to pass laws aimed at maximizing the pleasure and minimizing the pain of the largest number in society: "the greatest good for the greatest number" (1948, p. 151). If legislators are to legislate according to the principle of utility, said Bentham, they must understand human motivation and behavior, and for him, this was easily summed up:

> Nature has placed mankind under the governance of two sovereign masters, pain and pleasure. It is for them alone to point out what we ought to do, as well as to determine what we shall do. On the one hand the standard of right and wrong, on the other the chain of causes and effects, are fastened to their throne. They govern us in all we do, in all we say, in all we think: every effort we can make to throw off our subjection, will serve but to demonstrate and confirm it. (1948, p. 125).

In other words, if we are to understand any form of behavior at all and what motivates it, we have to do so with reference to those two "sovereign masters." That is, our efforts to maximize our pleasures and minimize our pains, whether in conforming or deviant ways, are really all we need to explain our behavior. This is the classical view of human nature, which in many ways mirrors the modern evolutionary view of human nature (minus the many nuances contained in evolutionary theory) that humans (and all animals) are designed to maximize their pleasure and minimize their pain. This design feature is an adaption and thus functional for the individual, but it can be socially disruptive if immediate concerns for gratification are placed above maintaining social harmony, and one seeks "money without work, sex without courtship, and revenge without court delays," as Gottfredson and Hirsch (1990, p. 89) put it. Collective social interests require limitations on self-interest. Thus, in the process of seeking individual interests, we must consider the pain and pleasure of others as well as the pains we ourselves might endure in the pursuit. Before we choose, we must consult the "standards of right and wrong" that are tied to the "throne" of individual pleasure seeking.

Plato's (1960) tripartite model of the soul (the psyche) is essentially about the hedonistic tug-of-war between the human capacities for good and evil and is an excellent source for understanding the struggle. Most of us play this tug-of-war with ourselves as we try to fulfill our needs while simultaneously staying within the bounds of socially acceptable actions. Plato's composite model of the soul consists of the appetitive soul, the rational soul, and the spirited soul. The appetitive soul motivates us to seek the pleasures necessary to sustain individual life and reproductive success (food, water, and sex) and is analogous to Freud's id. The rational soul is free-willed and urges us to make wise decisions when seeking our goals (Freud's ego), and the spirited soul (Freud's superego) values virtue, and in the good and wise person, it emotionally enforces the dictates of the rational soul. Plato explained his approach-avoid model of balancing behavior in the form of his allegory of the charioteer in which the charioteer is driving a chariot pulled by two winged horses, one white and one black. In the allegory, the charioteer is the rational soul fighting to control the emotional white horse and the appetitive black horse. As with Freud's id and superego, the black and white horses are pulling in opposite directions—the white horse toward the heavens and enlightenment, the black horse back toward the earth and the "despotic spirit."

Each horse has its strengths and weaknesses, and both are needed to move the chariot forward. The wise charioteer neither ignores nor indulges them, but harnesses them as a cooperative team. The white horse has an innate affinity for the charioteer and is commanded by the charioteer's word alone, but the black horse requires the whip to goad it in the right direction because it represents our innate and necessary needs. The charioteer only has to control the black horse; the white horse of his better nature knows the right way. If the black horse is allowed free reign, the person becomes an unabashed hedonist living only to fulfill the lust for pleasure. Freedom requires that the unruly black horse be reined in with a strong hand. If the black horse proves too strong for the charioteer and it rules the psyche, it will be able to enlist the emotional energy of the white horse to achieve its goals. If this occurs, instead of the noble emotions such as love and empathy dominating, the prominent emotions will be negative, such as lust, greed, anger, and resentment. Balancing the three parts is the secret behind a happy and successful prosocial life, and this can only be achieved by rationally making use of the strong arm of the charioteer using his agency to steer the chariot in a prosocial direction.

The Hedonistic Calculus

The classical explanation of criminal behavior and how to prevent it is derived from the Enlightenment assumption (which was identical with Plato's) that human nature is hedonistic, rational, and endowed with free will. In classical theory, individuals either obey or disobey the law according to the solutions they arrive at after engaging in hedonistic calculus. Hedonism is a doctrine whose central idea is that happiness (the satisfaction of desires) is the main goal of life. All other life goals are seen only as instrumentally desirable; that is, they are only desirable as means to the end of achieving pleasure or avoiding pain. Thus, hedonism is the greatest single motivator of human action. Of course, happiness and how to achieve it mean different things for different people, and the calculus of achievement depends on the intellectual resources one has to make it. We should not think of hedonism as the "folk-hedonism" of sex, drugs, and rock 'n' roll; that is, seeking immediate pleasure without regard for one's future well-being or for the well-being of others.

Rationality is behavior that is behavior consistent with logic. People are said to behave rationally when we observe a logical "fit" between the goals they strive for and the means they use to achieve them. The goal of human rationality is self-interest, and self-interest governs our behavior, whether in conforming or deviant directions. Bentham combined hedonism and rationality in the concept of the hedonistic calculus, a method by which individuals are assumed to logically weigh the anticipated benefits of a given course of action against its possible costs. If the balance of consequences of a contemplated action is thought to enhance pleasure and/or minimize pain, then individuals will pursue it; if not, they will not. In this view, human beings are endowed with free will which enables them to purposely and deliberately choose to follow a calculated course of action. Therefore, if people seek to increase their pleasures illegally or immorally, they do so freely and with full knowledge of the wrongness of their acts, and thus society has a legitimate right to punish those who harm others. It is acknowledged that free will and rationality are limited resources unevenly distributed in populations, but this observation, except in such circumstances as young age, or mental disease or defect, does not deny those attributes to any human being.

The Rise of Positivism

Just as the spirit of reason in the 18th century ushered in the classical school, the spirit of science in the second half of the 19th century ushered in the positivist school. The term "positivism" in the social sciences is used to designate the extension of the scientific method—from which more *positive* knowledge can be obtained—about social life. Positivists in the human sciences insisted on divorcing science from free will and morals and looking only at what is and not what ought to be. The writings of natural scientists, particularly those of Charles Darwin on evolution, generated a major new way of thinking about human nature just as revolutionary as the writings of the Enlightenment philosophers a century earlier. The flattering image of human beings that emerged from the Enlightenment gave way to the evolutionary view that we are different only in degree from other animal forms and that science could explain human behavior just as it could explain events in the nonhuman world. Positivist criminologists were more concerned with discovering biological, psychological, or sociological determinants of criminal behavior than with the classical concerns of legal and penal reforms.

Classicists defined criminal acts as natural consequences of the unrestrained human tendency to seek immediate pleasure, simple hedonistic abuses of free will. The problem with such an explanation, if accepted without qualification, is that it provides little possibility for further investigation. Thus, criminologists began to move away from the classical assumptions, especially the assumption of free will as it is commonly understood, and toward a more deterministic view of human behavior. This is not to say that hedonism, rationality, and free will are not human attributes. Rationality and free will may define the "essence" of human personhood because they are the attributes that most distinguish humans from other animals, but to accept these constructs in pure form as the sole reasons for behavior poses difficulties for science, which seeks measurable "causes" of phenomena that can be verified through replication.

The increasingly popular view among criminologists of this period was that crime resulted from internal and/or external forces impinging on individuals, biasing or even completely determining their behavioral choices. Enrico Ferri, one of the early positivists, gives us perhaps the best short description of the differences between classical and positivist criminology. Note that even back then criminologists from the different schools of thought were taking pot-shots at one another: We are empirical *scientists*; you pure deluded fools are just armchair philosophical *speculators* whose conclusions precede your inquiries:

> For them [the classicists] the facts should give place to syllogisms; for us [positivists] The facts govern and no reasoning can occur without starting from the facts. For them science only needs paper, pen, and ink and the rest comes from a Brain stuffed with … abundant reading of books. … For us science requires Spending a long time in examining the facts one by one, evaluating them, reducing them to a common denominator, [and] extracting the central idea from them. For them a syllogism or an anecdote suffices to demolish a myriad of facts gathered by years of observation and analysis; for us, the reverse is true. (in Curran & Renzetti, 2001, p. 16)

Ferri dismissed the notion of free will as a pernicious myth. For him, pre-positivistic notions of culpability, moral responsibility, and intent were to be subordinate to an assessment of the offender's strength of resistance to the criminal impulse (in this he appears to be consistent with Beccaria's notion of a despotic spirit that all humans are saddled with), with the express purpose of averting future danger to society. He believed that moral insensibility and lack of foresight, underscored by low intelligence, were the criminal's most marked characteristics: The criminal has "defective resistance to criminal tendencies and temptations, due to that ill–balanced impulsiveness which characterizes children and savages" (Ferri, 1917:11).

Biological Positivism: Cesare Lombroso and the Born Criminal

Five years after Charles Darwin published his *On the Origin of Species* proclaiming his theory of evolution by natural selection, Italian army physician and anthropologist Cesare Lombroso published *Criminal Man (*1876), which is considered the first book devoted solely to the causes of criminality ever written. Lombroso is widely acclaimed as the father of modern criminology, although he is often criticized for the racist and sexist views he expressed in his book. His basic idea was that some criminals (not all, as is commonly assumed) are born criminal. With his misunderstanding of Darwinian theory, he considered criminals to be evolutionary "throwbacks" to an earlier form of life. The term he used to describe the physical appearance of organisms said to resemble ancestral (prehuman) forms of life was "atavism." Lombroso was influenced by Ernst Haeckel's famous biogenetic law, which melodically states that "ontogeny recapitulates phylogeny." This "law," which is not entirely correct, states that individual organisms repeat in their ontogeny the same phases of evolution that their species underwent in its phylogeny. Criminals were thus considered by Lombroso to be "throwbacks" to a more primitive stage of evolution and could be identified by a number of measurable physical stigmata. These stigmata included protruding jaws, drooping eyes, large ears, twisted and flattish noses, long arms relative to the lower limbs, sloping shoulders, and a coccyx that resembled "the stump of a tail" (Lombroso-Ferrero, 1972, pp. 10–21).

This flawed concept of atavism highlights an important point of difference between the classical and positivist schools. Classical criminologists viewed criminals and non-criminals as essentially similar beings who simply freely chose different pathways in life, whereas positivists viewed them as being qualitatively different beings whose behavior was determined by their "beastly" natures. Lombroso was just one of many who sought to understand behavioral phenomena with reference to the principles of evolution as they were understood at the time. If humankind was just at one end of the continuum of animal life forms, it made sense to many people that criminals—who acted "beastly" and lacked reasoned conscience—were biologically inferior beings belonging to an earlier pre-civilized evolutionary period. As Mazzarello (2011) put it: "It was no longer free will that produced a deviant event, but the uncontrollable propulsive force emanating from the deepest instincts of a being arrested in an early stage of his biological evolution (p. 98)."

Bentham and Compatibilism

The sharp discontinuity between the classical and positivist schools we are often led to believe exists is not really the case, nor is it the case that all modern criminologist subscribes to determinism, at least not in the hard sense. Modern criminologists are divided in their beliefs about free will (or at least, compatibilism) and strict determinism. Richard Wright's (1995, p. 8) analysis of 53 criminology textbooks published from 1956 to 1965 and from 1983 to 1992 noted that "My data show that despite recent shifts in criminological theory toward a moderate view (reflecting the broader changes in sociology) that recognizes the importance of both deterministic and choice factors in criminal behavior, textbook authors during both periods tend to affirm a fairly rigid version of determinism when explaining crime." But this was by no means a consensus. Wright notes that in the earlier period 60.0% of texts embrace determinism, and 52.6%

of the texts in the latter period did so. My reading of explanations of criminality in more recent textbooks is that they are compatibilist rather than taking extreme positions on either free will or determinism.

The work of Jeremy Bentham may be considered a compatibilist bridge between the two early criminological schools. Despite Bentham's classical view of human nature, he never lost sight of its intricacies. While always maintaining the freedom of the will, he argued that the will was moved by "motives" arising from the "bodily senses," which were differentially felt by people according to certain internal and external factors. Estimates of the value of pleasures and pains are to be considered with reference to four circumstances: intensity (severity), duration, certainty, and propinquity (how soon after some action is taken is the pleasure or pain forthcoming) (Bentham, 1948).

In expressing these views, Bentham added certain nuances about human nature to classical theory that did not contradict its assumptions regarding free will and rationality. He devoted an entire chapter of *A Fragment on Government* to 32 biological, psychological, and social factors (e.g., intelligence, temperament, personality, gender, age, education, occupation) that he thought of as "circumstances influencing sensibility" (1948: Chapter VI). Bentham did not assume that people are completely free because these factors constrain choices, but within those constraints, people still have many choices. Every human action is a combination of free action and necessity, both of which differ in the degree to which they have power depending on circumstances. Although he only devoted a single paragraph to each of these influences, the fact that he recognized internal and external constraints on free will and rationality (note, however, that he uses the term "influencing" not "determining") leads us to suppose that Bentham may be considered both the last of the "pure" Beccarian classical criminologists and the first of the positivist criminologists.

Chapter Seven

Returning to Classic Assumptions of Human Nature

An About-Turn on Positivism

The positivist school of criminology held a tight rein in criminology for almost a century after its emergence by emphasizing science and rejecting metaphysical assumptions about human nature, such as rationality and free will. Criminology was born out of that rejection (Hirschi, 2017). However, a combination of climbing crime rates, the failure of existing theories to adequately account for them, and the emergence of more conservative attitudes in the late 1970s to early 1980s saw a swing away from the ideals of positivism back to the classical notion that offenders are rational actors responsible for their own actions. Positivists continued to reject the idea, however, reasoning that individuals cannot be both subject to biological or social-structural causation and freely choose their actions. The idea that people make choices was viewed as a threat to their commitment to environmental causation, which Robert Sampson (2012, p. 374) could not understand: "there is something odd about the way many social scientists approach individual choice, almost as if they are spooked into thinking that choice renders the environment impotent." Nigel Pleasants (2019, p. 4) likewise does not believe that choice renders the environment impotent, but believes that "social structure conditions and influences, but does not determine, agents' choices." Moreover, he argues that social structure is dependent on human agency:

> It is widely acknowledged that human agency is a necessary condition for the existence and functioning of social structure. "Social structures," [critical realist philosopher Roy Bhaskar] proclaims, "exist only in virtue of, and are exercised only in, human agency," and are "concept dependent," that is, operate only via people's understandings of their activities and relations with one another. Because of these features of its ontology, structurationists maintain that social structure can only influence or condition action, not determine it. (p. 7; internal citations omitted)

One of the principal complaints made by conservative criminologists such as Hirschi and Hindelang (1977), Hirschi (2017), Wilson (1975), and Wilson & Herrnstein (1985) was that many criminological theories want to trace "root causes" of crime to society and to exonerate delinquents and criminals from any blame for their actions. According to them, viewing offenders as blameless strips them of their humanity and paints them as pawns of capricious environmental winds, and leads offenders to view themselves as victims, a deadly trap from which they may never escape. To illustrate such attitudes, Boyd Sharp (2006, p. xvi) cited a Calvin and Hobbes cartoon in which Calvin says: "I have concluded that nothing bad I do is my fault … being young and irresponsible I'm a helpless victim of countless bad influences.

An unwholesome culture panders to my undeveloped values and it pushes me into misbehavior. I take no responsibility for my behavior. I'm an innocent pawn of society."

Sharp's point is that oftentimes criminals come to think like Calvin (who obviously has an external locus of control) in the context of a society where many people prefer to claim victimhood rather than personal responsibility (McDonald's made me fat, the Marlboro man made me smoke, I steal because I'm deprived, and so forth). This kind of externality of blame and denial of personal agency is called "skinkin' thinkin'" in corrections. Criminals are eager to accept authoritative pronouncements by criminologists that excuse their behavior, and defense lawyers are equally quick to argue them in court. All of this reinforces the patterns of criminal denial that treatment providers in corrections (prison counselors, probation and parole officers, and social workers) find so frustrating (Walsh & Stohr, 2010). Thus, there were a variety of reasons that many of the classical ideas about criminal offending reemerged when they did.

Rational Choice Theory

Two popular theories based on neoclassical ideas of human nature are rational choice theory and routine activities theory. The most common thread of the two theories is the emphasis on the roles of criminal situations and opportunities and the ratio of benefits to risks in making decisions about whether to engage in criminal behavior (the hedonistic calculus). This is in stark contrast with most other theories that focus on criminal offenders' personality characteristics such as impulsiveness, intelligence, negative emotionality, and callousness, or social statuses such as race, class, poverty, gender, and age. These theories see the relationship between choice and causality as one of elucidating the conditions under which people are able to exercise their free will. Jock Young states that "The structure of my argument is that, given that human beings are culture-creating beings and are endowed with free will, albeit in circumstances not of their own making, the verstehen of human meaning is, by definition, a necessity in any explanation of human activity, criminal or otherwise" (2016, p. 27). Thus, rational choice and routine activities theories focus on the process of individual choices to commit a crime within the immediate circumstances surrounding a criminal event.

According to Milos Krstić (2022, p. 10): "Rational choice theory is, at its foundation, a simple action theory that allows us to understand how 'aspects' of a social situation can affect the choices and actions of individuals. As a normative theory, it tells us what we need to do to achieve our goals as much as possible." Rational choice theory is based on the basic tenets of classical theory that maintains that people choose their behavior and that they do so motivated by the hedonistic calculus. It does so, however, with the added concern for the immediate social context. For rational choice theorists, all behavior, good or bad, is designed to produce some net advantage for the actor, and because people are rational, they will respond to incentives and disincentives in such a way as to maximize pleasure and minimize pain. Or expressed less strongly: "people act within the limits of their abilities to pursue what they perceive as most satisfying" (Ward, Stafford, & Gray, 2006, p. 572).

Criminal behavior, like any other behavior, is motivated by many things. It could be anger, greed, lust, thrills, jealousy, revenge, status, peer approval, or any number of other reasons. Whatever the reason, at bottom it is all about attempts to gain some sort of personal satisfaction (pleasure) or to remove some source of irritation (pain). This does not mean that rational choice theorists harbor extreme libertarian notions of a will free of any causal chains. Rational choice theorists are compatibilists because while they believe that criminal behavior is ultimately a choice, the choice is made in the context of personal abilities and disabilities and situational constraints and opportunities. They realize that people's free will do not create the multiple possibilities available to them, but they still may capitalize on them. Rational choice theorists thus substitute libertarian free will for the concept of human agency.

Human agency is a notion that maintains humans have the capacity to make choices and the responsibility to make moral ones regardless of internal or external constraints impinging on them. Robert Agnew asks if it is

> appropriate to hold individuals accountable for their agentic behavior when the ability and inclination to exercise agency may be determined by forces beyond their control? I would respond by stating that while individuals may have no control over those factors that contribute to the exercise of agency, agency still involves the ability to make and act on choices that are not fully determined by forces beyond the individual's control. Agentic individuals therefore have the ability—to varying degrees—to choose crime or conventional behavior. As such, they still bear some responsibility for their behavior. (2013, p. 87)

Agency is thus a form of free will that is compatible with soft determinism in that it recognizes both the internal and external constraints that limit our ability to do as we might please. Rational choice theorists acknowledge the variety of forces influencing our decisions and behavior, and that these are beyond our control, but these influences limit, but do not eliminate, our freedom to decide how we will behave. They also acknowledge that the strength and persistence of these limitations within which we exercise free will differs among people. Those experiencing more constraints will have a lower degree of freedom available to them thus making moral decisions more difficult. That said, even those experiencing the most difficult of hardships still maintain agency. Because rational choice theory grants offenders the dignity of possessing agency, just as non-offenders weigh options before deciding on an important course of action, so do offenders before deciding to commit a crime, and therefore: "He or she can be held responsible for that choice and can be legitimately punished" (Clarke & Cornish, 2001, p. 25).

Rationality

Rationality is a defining quality of human beings. The basic notion is that rationality is the ability to deliberate on available behavioral options with good sense and sound judgment. Good sense and sound judgment are said to be present when we base our choices on the evidence before us at any given time, and when we revise our reasoning and the behavior it motivates as new evidence arises. Rationality is not to be confused with morality because rationality's goal is self-interest, and self-interest governs behavior whether in conforming or deviant directions. Crime is rational (at least in the short run) if criminals employ reason and act purposely to gain desired ends. Travis Hirschi's control theory views people as rationally weighing their options: "In social control theory, actors weigh the costs and benefits of alternative lines of action, legal and illegal, and choose those they consider most likely to maximize their pleasure" (Hirschi, 2017, p. 108). Rationality is thus the quality of thinking and behaving in accordance with logic and reason such that one's reality is an ordered and intelligible system for achieving goals.

Rationality engages the free will/determinism argument. When people deliberate about whether to do something or not, it follows that they believe that it is within their power to choose one option over another. Such a belief conflicts with determinism, which rules out options; that is, a belief that one can rationally deliberate on alternative choice of action would be inconsistent with the notion that there are no conditions under which one could have done otherwise than one did. Thus, if a person believes that he or she can rationally deliberate on alternative behaviors and at the same time believes that his or her behavior is fully determined by factors other than self, then he or she holds contradictory beliefs. That person would be like the person who denies free will: "anyone who denies the existence of free will must inevitably, contradict himself with monotonous regularity" (van Inwagen, 1983, p. 160). Van Inwagen is making the point that people cannot live their determinism, try as they may.

It does seem that a belief in determinism undermines our ability to think of ourselves as agents who deliberate rationally. But it is the belief in the hard determinism of many criminological theories that undermine this ability, not the soft determination of rational choice theory that emphasizes "influence" rather than "cause." Although hard criminological theories do not explicitly state it, they imply that rational deliberation is incompatible with their notions of determinism. Derk Pereboom offers a solution to this issue in what he calls "deliberation compatibilism" to this apparent paradox and defines it thus: "Deliberation-compatibilism: S's deliberating and being rational is compatible with S's believing that her actions are causally determined" (2008, p. 288). Because the term "cause" contains a lot of philosophical baggage, I would amend Pereboom slightly to read: "S's deliberating and being rational is compatible with S's believing that there were sufficient antecedent conditions that are not within her control that accounted for her actions."

The concept of rationality in the social sciences is indebted to German economist and sociologist Max Weber. Weber conceived of two broad types of rationality. The first is *zweckrationalitat* ("purpose" or "instrumental" rationality) which is self-serving means-ends rationality that Weber assumed to be innate: "personal self-interest is already fixed by genetic inheritance in all human individuals and needs no further fixing there by external imposition" (in Wallace, 1990, p. 209). Purposive means-ends rational action was central to Weber's methodological individualism form of sociological analysis. Weber agreed with classical scholars that rationality is a part of human nature that is pressed into service to assure that we meet goals that serve our interests. The second form is learned rationality or *wertrationalitat* ("value" rationality). This type of rationality is related to a value such as honor or to duty to some revered entity (one's nation, group, God, etc.) or idea (patriotism, ideology, religion, etc.), which may appear to others as antithetical to instrumental rationality. *Zweckrationalitat* thus points us to reasoned means of attaining goals, and *wertrationalitat* helps to define those motives, means, and goals in terms of the norms and values of our social groups.

Just as there are limits to free will, there are limits to rationality. A rational decision is one that is reasoned to be optimal for achieving a goal, but rationality is subjective and bounded. Given that it is subjective and bounded, unwanted outcomes can be produced by seemingly rational strategies. This is because we do not all make the same calculations or arrive at the same plan when pursuing the same goals. We all contemplate our anticipated actions with imperfect knowledge, with different mindsets and different reasoning abilities. In other words, we may think that we are behaving in ways that best serve our self-interest, but our behavior may bring unwanted results because we are ignorant of some things and misinterpret others. We do the best we can to order our decisions relating to our self-interest with the knowledge and understanding we have about the possible outcomes of a particular course of action. All people have mental models of the world and behave rationally with respect to them, even if others might consider our behavior to be irrational. Criminals behave rationally from their limited subjective models of reality, and "are generally doing the best they can within the limits of time, resources, and information available to them. This is why we characterize their decision making as rational, albeit in a limited way" (Clarke & Cornish, 2001, p. 25).

Rather than focusing on the personality traits and social backgrounds of criminals, rational choice theorists simply assume criminally motivated offenders will always be with us and focus on the process of their choices to offend (the foreground rather than the background of crime). This process is known as choice structuring, defined as "the constellation of opportunities, costs, and benefits attaching to particular kinds of crime" (Cornish & Clarke, 1987, p. 993). We all make choices all the time, but making good ones that maximize the probability that they will result in the desired outcome requires a strategy that structures them. Experienced burglars, for instance, have to take a variety of factors into consideration before burglarizing a home. They will already have in their heads a general strategy about where to go, when to go, and what to do to successfully burgle a house that structures their thinking. Thus, criminal events require motivated offenders meeting situations that they perceive as an opportunity to acquire something they want. Each criminal event is the result of a series of choice structuring decisions to initiate the event, continue with it, or desist. Each particular kind of crime is the result of a series of different decisions that can only be explained on their own terms.

Routine Activities Theory

Routine activities theory was devised by Lawrence Cohen and Marcus Felson (1979) in the tradition of rational choice theory and attempts to explain crime rates in different societies and neighborhoods without invoking individual differences in criminal propensity. They do this by pointing to the routine activities in that society or neighborhood. Routine activities are defined as "recurrent and prevalent activities which provide for basic population and individual needs" (Cohen & Felson, 1979, p. 593). That is, routine activities are the normal day-to-day activity patterns that characterize a particular place that either invite or dissuade crime. Take, for example, the significant increase in the burglary rate in the United States in the 1960s. According to Cohen & Felson (1979), this was almost entirely attributable to the increasing numbers of women entering the workforce, which meant that there were fewer people at home to guard it, and thus more opportunities for criminals as homes "routinely" were left unoccupied during the day. Routine activities theorists decline to take a position on free will, but they do assert that offenders are rational, albeit in a limited sense.

Routine activities theory discounts what others see as causes of crime such as poverty and inequality, pointing out that crime increased dramatically with the expansion of the welfare state from the 1960s onwards which was supposed to address these things (Walsh & Ellis, 2007). Society's affluence is as much a "cause" of crime as its poverty because affluence brings with it many opportunities for crime to occur. Of course, it's not that the average affluent person commits more crimes than the average poor person; rather, a general level of affluence makes more things available to obtain illegally. Additionally, convenience stores and ATM machines competing for their share of the general affluence stay open all hours of the day and night, thus making them convenient for robbers and thieves as well as for shoppers. An affluent society offers many targets for the not-so-affluent who want "their share" of the pie. Increased crime may be the price we have to pay for increased affluence.

According to Cohen and Felson (1979), crime is the result of (1) motivated offenders meeting (2) suitable targets that lack (3) capable guardians. If these three elements do not converge in time and space, crime is not likely to occur. Motivated offenders are individuals willing to make criminal choices when an opportunity presents itself. Suitable targets are persons or places that offenders view as vulnerable or attractive and who possess something that they want or objects that they want to possess. Capable guardians are persons (mates, friends, patrolling police, concerned neighbors, and so on) or things (alarms, locked doors, well-lit streets, etc.) that deter criminal activity. For instance, unmarried females living alone are more likely victimized both for personal and property crimes because they are likely to be out alone at night (in bars, at home alone, or walking alone) and they lack anyone to help in guarding themselves or their property.

Cohen and Felson take motivated offenders for granted and do not attempt to explain their existence. The theory is thus very much like rational choice theory in that it describes situations in which criminal victimization is likely to occur. In poor disorganized communities, there is never a shortage of motivated offenders, and although the pickings are generally slim in such areas, victimization is more prevalent in them than in more affluent areas. High victimization rates in poor disorganized areas are the result of both a plentiful supply of motivated offenders living in them and residents of such areas often tend to lack capable guardians for their persons or their property. Because of disrupted families, transient neighbors, poverty, and all the other negative aspects of disorganized neighborhoods, except for police patrols, capable guardians are in short supply. Crime rates can go up or down depending on how routine activities change without any changes in offender motivation or in the prevalence of motivated offenders.

Criticisms of Rational Choice

Both rational choice and routine activities theories resonate most with conservative criminologists who maintain that offenders are thinking agents who must be held responsible for their criminal choices regardless of the external influences that impinge on them. Although this position grants criminals the dignity of having reasoned control over their lives, many criminologists tend not to like it because it leads to a retributivist stance on punishment and ignores distal causes of crime and the need for rehabilitation (Lilly, Cullen & Ball, 2011). However, the flip side to this is that rehabilitation requires the rejection of an external locus of control and of the kind of "stinkin' thinkin'" victim self-identity of people like Calvin and the acceptance of personal responsibility, although it is true that it does lead to a just deserts retributivist stance on punishment.

The assumption that rational choice explain criminal behavior is the criticism most often leveled at rational choice theory, however. It is assumed that everyone agrees that all humans of sound mind are rational in the classical sense of wanting to optimize satisfactory outcomes resulting from their choices. But if every person of sound mind is rational, rationality is a constant and constants cannot explain variables. Thus, rational choice cannot by itself explain something as variable as human behavior. What we need to adequately explain behavior are the factors that affect offenders' rationality but do not affect non-offenders' rationality, or vice versa.

Walsh and Jorgensen (2020) compare the choices that billionaire Bill Gates and the infamous criminal Charlie Manson made in their lives and ask:

> what leads people like Charlie Manson to decide, quite rationally, that increasing his pleasure means immediate gratification (a drug fix now, a woman for tonight) and minimizing his pain (boredom, drug craving) are best met by robbery and other crimes, while people like Bill Gates decide, just as rationally, that his needs are best met by delaying gratification, attending college, getting a good job, getting married and settling down? (p. 91)

Gates' rationality was oriented toward the future; the long-term consequences of his choices, while Manson's rationality was oriented to present satisfaction. This orientation to the resent is typical of many criminals, and thus it would seem that the typical criminal's rationality is severely bounded. We continually see more than two-thirds of released criminals being returned to prison, and that is hardly maximizing pleasure and minimizing pain (Stohr & Walsh, 2019). Criminals are rational from their own limited point of view, and they do sometimes deliberate on the costs and benefits of their actions, but like the rest of us, criminals are not walking calculating machines who routinely take time to weigh the pros and cons of their every move. As van den Haag (2003, p. 247) puts it: "Law abiding people habitually ignore criminal opportunities. Law breakers habitually discount the risk of punishment. Neither calculates." Be this as it may, it is doubtful if even habitual criminals walk blindly into a crime without any calculating at all. Even though it is true that few people ever commit a serious crime, anyone may be tempted to commit a crime if the ratio of benefit to cost is high, and habitual criminals do not just bump into criminal opportunities; they actively create them.

Despite many well-argued criticisms of rational choice, we can still think of rational free will as the ability to choose how we will behave from a range of available alternatives. Bill Gates' alternatives were far greater than Charles Manson's, but I doubt that anyone really believes that Manson had no other possible alternatives than crime and that therefore his criminal actions were compelled. It may be quite true that those who lead law-abiding lives had more alternatives in their life choices than those who do not but to say that criminals had *no* other alternative than crime is disingenuous. No doubt we can articulate causes for the criminal's actions, but this hardly presents a problem. All human actions are influenced by multiple factors, but none of them are necessary and sufficient to account for the actor's conscious rational decision to commit or desist from committing crimes. We realize that the criminal's agential decision had to be triggered by factors external to him and prior to his reflective choice, because these external factors did not arise from his reflections, and he can only choose options that are available to him. Nevertheless, his reflection on those factors, his interpretation of them, and the choice he made is a vital link in the chain that led to the outcome. Criminals are not preprogrammed automatons; they possess the necessary faculties to know the difference between right and wrong and have the ability to resist acts that are contrary to civilized society.

Chapter Eight

The Origin and Purpose of Punishment

The Co-Evolution of Punishment and Social Cooperation

Nathaniel Hawthorne's opening words of his 1850 novel *The Scarlet Letter* are: "The founders of a new colony, whatever Utopia of human virtue and happiness they might originally project, have invariably recognized it among their earliest practical necessities to allot a portion of the virgin soil as a cemetery, and another portion as the site of a prison" (2003, p. 1). Hawthorne is reminding us of two things we cannot avoid—death and human malfeasance—and that any established community must make provisions for both. In his *Division of Labor in Society*, Emile Durkheim (1997) also noted that crime is a universal feature of all societies and that it serves a vital social function through the ritual of punishing criminals. It is by such punishment that the moral boundaries of society are clearly demarcated and attachment to those boundaries reinforced. For Durkheim, the purpose of punishment is to strengthen social solidarity by group expression of moral outrage and to reaffirm the justness of social norms and the moral commitment of the law-abiding. He also maintained that the urge to punish is inherent in human nature and that it soothes, pacifies, and provides feelings of satisfaction when a wrongdoer is punished.

The urge to punish wrongdoers is universal and strong (Penney, 2012), so punishment must have been evolutionarily adaptive. The evolutionary importance of punishment is not as obvious as the procurement of vital resources or sexual partners, but we still find pleasure when wrongdoers are punished. Brain imaging studies have shown increased blood flow to various reward areas of the brain when subjects witness the punishment of those who have wronged them (de Quervain et al., 2004; Klein, 2012). Blood flow to reward centers has also been observed when people who have harmed other people are punished, and the strength of the pleasure response is proportional both to the harm done and to the level of the offender's culpability (whether the act was purposeful, knowing, reckless, or negligent) (Buckholtz & Marois, 2012). These imaging studies provide us with some compelling evidence that the urge to punish must be an adaptive feature of human nature and explains the old saying "vengeance is sweet."

There must be good evolutionary reasons why our reward centers fire when we witness the punishment (vicariously via the news media) of wrongdoers, but this observation does not reveal why punishment was so vital to our distant ancestors' survival and reproductive goals that it led to selection for such neural responses. We may start by noting that *Homo sapiens* is an ultra-social species that alone among all animals lives in large groups consisting overwhelmingly of non-kin. We live under an implied social contract by which we surrender some of our freedoms to do as we please. A vital part of the contract is the agreement not to harm others, and if we do, the group, or in modern times, the state, has the legitimate right to punish us. As Keally McBride opines: "Punishment is the midwife in the birth of the social contract" (2007, p. 122).

The most primitive form of state punishment is "eye-for-an-eye" retribution. Few people in modern Western societies advocate such literal practices, but retribution, or punishment that is justly deserved for its own sake, still has wide purchase. In his dissenting opinion in *Furman v. Georgia* in which the U.S. Supreme Court invalidated Georgia's death penalty statute in 1972, Justice Potter Stewart wrote the following regarding retribution:

> I cannot agree that retribution is a constitutionally impermissible ingredient in the imposition of punishment. The instinct for retribution is part of the nature of man, and channeling that instinct in the administration of criminal justice serves an important purpose in promoting the stability of a society governed by law. When people begin to believe that organized society is unwilling or unable to impose upon criminal offenders the punishment they "deserve," then there are sown the seeds of anarchy—of self-help, vigilante justice, and lynch law.

If retribution is part of the "nature of man," what are the selective pressures that led to its evolution? The evolutionary goals of all sexually reproducing animals are survival and reproduction, and it is important that they be motivated to take action in the pursuit of these goals. To produce such motivation, nature has provided us with a built-in biological system that rewards us with pleasurable feelings when we do things that aid in achieving these goals. Such pleasurable feelings arise from dopamine attaching to the brain's reward centers (Walsh, Johnson, & Bolen, 2012). Each surge of dopamine reinforces the behavior that makes us feel good and motivates us to repetition. This is why we feel so good when we satisfy urges to eat, drink, and have sex, which are the most obvious requirements for survival and reproduction.

To survive harsh evolutionary environments, humans had to evolve strong norms of cooperation. The natural selection for altruism is adequate to understand cooperation among close kin for whom we have strong emotional feelings, but it does not explain cooperation extended to non-kin. Cooperation among non-kin is explained by reciprocal altruism—the extending of a benefit to another with the unspoken expectation of obtaining a benefit from the recipient at a later date. Social animals cooperate because they can achieve more as a group than they can individually, and we feel good when helping others. Even if the person we help is a stranger whom we are unlikely to encounter again, our brains still receive a shot of dopamine that makes us feel good (Brunero, 2002). Brain imaging studies consistently show that our pleasure centers "light up" when either giving or receiving something valued, but brain areas associated with the pleasures of social attachments only fire when giving (Moll et al., 2006).

However, a population of cooperators provides a target-rich niche for people who cheat on the social contract and gain resources at zero cost. Cheats prosper in a population of unconditional cooperators (biologists call them "suckers)" and would soon drive them to extinction. Most humans are not suckers; they are conditional cooperators, or what biologists call "grudgers." Grudgers can be cheated because they abide by the norms of mutual trust and cooperation and expect the same from others. Unlike suckers, once cheated grudgers will react differently to cheaters in the future by not offering them cooperation (Wiebe, 2011). The theft of resources and sexual mates in evolutionary environments posed a severe threat to everyone in the group, and thus would have generated feelings of anger, outrage, and a desire to punish. As de Waal points out: "A taste of revenge is the other side of the coin of reciprocity" (1996, p. 160).

Victims feel angry and hurt when treated unfairly, and frustrated when the expectation of reciprocity is violated. Without moral outrage, there would be no motivation to react against those who violate the norms of reciprocal cooperation, and cheats would have thrived without the threat of punishment in our ancestral environments (Haidt, 2001). But natural selection does not pass judgment on emotions but on the *consequences* of behavior motivated by the emotion (Massey, 2002). It is no use feeling angry and hurt when victimized if those feelings do not generate behavior designed to prevent further occurrence. Negative feelings accompanying victimization are lessened by punishing violators because punishment signals the restoration of fairness and predictability (the perception that cheaters may be deterred from future cheating). The positive feelings accompanying the punishment of those who have wronged us, coupled with the reduction of negative feelings, provide powerful reinforcement for punitive responses.

Second- and Third-Party Punishment

Crime victims generally do not punish their victimizers themselves today, and even in evolutionary environments, it was probably more prudent to turn to others to carry the burden. Among primates, particularly among chimpanzees, alpha males take on the role of what is called *control behavior*, which includes the punishment of troop members who bully and exploit others (de Waal, 1996). As arbiters, alpha males typically show a preference for the weaker party in most disputes. This develops support among the weaker rank and file and serves to level the hierarchy and thereby increasing the gap between the alpha male and the more powerful members of the group who might seek to replace him (de Waal, 1996). Computer simulation studies of human altruistic punishment (punishment on behalf of others) have conclusively shown that the punisher receives many benefits, including an increased likelihood of receiving future benefits, with enhanced status in the group being the most valuable (Ule et al., 2009). Dos Santos, Rankin, and Wedekind remark that "reputation is the key to the evolution of punishment, and that simple reputation games can explain the high preservation of punishment in humans" (2011, p. 376).

In modern societies, punishment is meted out by third parties not directly harmed who will not directly benefit (like second-party chimp alpha males) from meting out punishment. Third-party punishers are the agents of the state operating under the law. Numerous experiments have shown that third parties motivated by compassion will punish cheats, even at a cost to themselves. In a novel dual brain EEG scanning model of 42 subjects in which dyadic interaction between two brains is measured simultaneously, Ciaramidaro et al. (2018) demonstrated that subjects showed a strong willingness to punish cheats, and the more unfair the cheating, the stronger the punishment "points" allotted to the cheater. These researchers noted: "Compassion is a particular form of empathic reaction to harm that befalls others and is accompanied by a desire to alleviate their suffering. This altruistic behavior is often manifested through altruistic punishment, wherein individuals penalize a deprecated human's actions, even if they are directed toward strangers." Henrich et al. (2006, p. 1770) note that: "societies with high degrees of punishment will also exhibit more altruistic behavior." This suggests that punishment and altruism co-evolved: "third-party punishment of norm violations ('I punish you because you harmed him') seems especially crucial for the evolutionary stability of cooperation and is the cornerstone of modern models of criminal justice" (Buckholtz & Marois, 2012, p. 655).

Free Mind and Punishment Justifications

The issue of free will and responsibility is the theme of many debates about punishment. Punitive decisions in the criminal justice system depend on the notion that a criminal before the court should have acted differently. This presupposes that he *could* have acted differently. This is a presupposition that legal systems around the world operate with except in rare circumstances when the offender's mind is severely compromised by brain abnormalities such as tumors. But there are those who want to mitigate, or even withhold punishment under the belief that behavior is fully determined by outside circumstances such as poverty and/or some genetic polymorphism statistically linked to a greater probability of offending. However, the law maintains that almost all criminals are at least minimally rational, possess the necessary faculties to know the difference between right and wrong, and have the ability to resist acting on aspects of their natures that are contrary to civilized society. Those who wish to abandon punishment on the grounds that it "dehumanizes" criminals evidently have no problem dehumanizing them by stripping them of their rationality and free mind.

Even though we assume that society has a right and a duty to punish those who harm others, it is in need of ethical justification. Any philosophy of punishment involves defining the concept of punishment and the values, attitudes, and beliefs contained in that definition, as well as justifying the imposition of a painful burden on someone. Punishment justifications—deterrence, incapacitation, rehabilitation, and retribution—come and go in popularity depending on the ideology of the times. When we speak of justifying something, we mean that we must provide reasons for doing it both in terms of morality ("It's the right thing to do") and in terms of the goals we wish to achieve ("Do this, and we'll get that"). In other words, we expect that punishment has favorable consequences that justify its application. Deterrence, incapacitation, and rehabilitation justifications are consequentialist in that they claim that punishment is morally justified if it produces beneficial consequences; that is, punishment is a means to an end. Retribution is non-consequentialist in that it justifies punishment by its intrinsic moral worth regardless of any benefits that may derive from it (Wood, 2010).

Deterrence has long been considered the primary function of punishment. It assumes that humans are rational actors who chose their behaviors in accordance with the hedonistic calculus and weigh the punishment they may receive for committing a crime against the benefits they might obtain by committing it. Deterrence assumes that there would be more crime and antisocial behavior than is now the case if people did not fear the possibility of punishment. Deterrence believers must thus believe in at least weak forms of rationality and free mind.

Incapacitation refers to the inability of criminals to victimize people outside prison walls while imprisoned. The justification for incapacitation is summarized by James Q. Wilson: "Wicked people exist. Nothing avails except to set them apart from innocent people" (1975, p. 391). It is obvious that incapacitation "works" while criminals are incarcerated. For instance, criminologist Elliot Currie (1989) tells us that in 1985 there were 135,000 inmates in prison whose most serious crime was robbery, and that each robber averages five robberies per year. Had these robbers not been imprisoned, they might have been responsible for an additional 135,000 × 5 or 675,000 robberies on top of the 580,000 actual robberies reported to the police that year.

Rehabilitation means restoring to constructive or healthy activity. It is more forward-looking to offenders' future behavior than backward-looking at what they have done. The rehabilitative goal is based on a model championed by people who view criminal behavior as analogous to sickness requiring treatment. Rehabilitation treatment models all assume that it is possible for criminals to shed their "stinkin' thinkin'" and accept responsibility for their actions. It is thus no accident that criminals with an internal locus of control evidence better readiness, amenability to and engagement with treatment, and better treatment outcomes than those with an external locus of control (reviewed in Tyler, Heffernan, & Fortune, 2020). Hard determinists would say that the treatment "caused" the positive outcomes, which is true in the sense that the rehabilitative outcome would probably not have occurred in the absence of treatment, but the fact remains that it was treatment, plus offenders' decisions to engage with it and profit from it, that resulted in the outcome. Treatment can cause nothing by itself.

Retribution differs from other punishment justifications in maintaining that punishment for its own sake is morally justified. Most criminologists abhor retribution as little more than state-sanctioned revenge (Rosebury, 2009), although a number of states such as California have explicitly embraced retribution in theircriminal codes (California Penal Code Sec. 1170a): "The Legislature finds and declares that the purpose of imprisonment for a crime is punishment" (in Barker, 2006, p. 12). Following German philosopher Immanuel Kant, retributionists argue that punishment is morally justified in terms of the value, dignity, and agency of human beings. Humans, says Kant (1964), are different from other animals because they are guided by reason, and it is from reason that we derive all duties and obligations. Humans have a duty to act out of reverence for moral law, which Kant conceived of as a set of categorical imperatives which state that an act should be done "in itself" regardless of any end. In other words, a categorical imperative says "Do this," not "Do this *if*." Any action consistent with this is moral, says Kant, regardless of its consequences. Kant says that a categorical imperative should be grounded in something that should be an end in itself and an absolute value. He finds this grounding in "man," who "exists as an end in himself, not merely as a means for arbitrary use for this or that will" (1964, p. 95). "Man," in all his actions, must always be regarded as an end in himself regardless of whether his actions are directed at himself or at others: "Act in such a way that you always treat humanity, whether in your own person or in the person of any other, never simply as a means, but always at the same time as an end" (1964, p. 96).

Respecting humans as ends in themselves led Kant to a retributionist justification of punishment. He maintained that punishment for instrumental reasons such as deterrence or rehabilitation is morally wrong because it treats people as *means* to an end, not as *ends in themselves.* Kant maintained that criminals are ruled by reason like everyone else and thus must live in accordance with universal moral standards ("Act as if the maxim of your action were to become through your will a universal law of nature"). By punishing criminals, the state is treating them in accordance with their own maxims; that is, how they think others should be treated. The state is thus allowing criminals to decide how they will be treated, and by doing so it is respecting their judgment and autonomy: "His own evil deed draws the punishment upon himself" (Rachels, 1986, p. 123). Retribution is thus a "just deserts" model demanding that criminals be punished in proportion to the harm they have done. Logan and Gaes (1993) claim that this is the most honest justification for punishment because it taps into our punitive urges and posits no secondary purpose for it, and they mirror Kant in writing that only retributive punishment "is an affirmation of the autonomy, responsibility, and dignity of the individual" (p. 252).

A retributive punishment justification is the only justification associated with deep emotions. When people hear of some vicious criminal act, they become angry, outraged, and disgusted, and their first inclination is to want to exact some sort of retribution; it is highly unlikely that their first thoughts should be of deterrence or rehabilitation. Rob Canton (2015,

p. 59) insists that "the emotions of punishment are distinctly *moral* emotions. They are emotions of judgment, of righteousness and reprobation." Writing of care and compassion, Canton remarks, "retributive emotions reflect a decent compassion for a victim's distress and a virtuous expression of solidarity with members of our community" (p. 62). Retribution engages the deep instinct of fairness, and "restores a balance: the offender's unjust profit or gain from the crime must be redressed or annulled. … The retributivist does not hit, but *hits back*" (p. 63). Canton says that the urge to punish can be seen as loyalty to the group and an expression of commitment to it. Offenders are subconsciously viewed as enemies of the group which serves to neutralize our feelings of care and compassion for them. Many people are disturbed by the retributionist's emotion-based justification for punishment, yet are emotionally disturbed themselves when they perceive innocent people are being punished. Why then do they consider it wrong when the same emotional outrage is aimed at the acts of criminals? If the moral judgment in the first instance is virtuous, then it is also virtuous in the second instance.

Against Punishment

A number of thinkers take a hard determinist position on criminal culpability, and hence against punishing them. The criminal lawyer Clarence Darrow is reputed to have said that criminals act when committing crimes only in the same sense as they do "when cut by bleeding" (in Walsh, 1981, p. 70). Darrow believed that they could no more command their behavior than they could command their wounds to stop bleeding. Likewise, psychiatrist Karl Menninger (1968) believed that criminals are not purposefully bad individuals who deserve punishment. He further argued that the practice of punishment itself is a crime against humanity because society is harming those it calls criminal when they are sick and require treatment. Along similar lines, Michael Zimmerman (2011) maintains that people should be held responsible and punished only for behavior they can control, but seems to consider most criminal behavior to be beyond the control of the criminal, and presumably, he believes should not be punished for such crimes. Similarly, Gregg Caruso (2021, p. 123) wants to apply a public health model to our response to criminals because "free will skepticism maintains that criminals are not morally responsible for their actions in the basic desert sense."

Likewise, Reznik (2019, p. 154) urges us to abolish punishment, which "requires an abandonment of 'the very concept of crime, as wrongdoing to which the community should respond with condemnation,' substituting it with a private conflict between members of the community that is a mere civil matter." He is not alone in this sentiment. Bagaric, Hunter, and Svilar (2021, p. 367) note that "A popular proposed alternative to the institution of punishment is to treat what are presently categorized as criminal acts in the same manner as civil wrongs, where the emphasis is on reconciliation and reparation." Turning crimes into torts would mean that the beaten mugging victim can sue his or her victim in civil court for monetary damages; good luck on getting a robber who claims poverty as the cause of his crimes to cough up. And what reconciliation can the parents get with a man who raped and murdered their child, and how can such evil be repaired? Furthermore, it would be morally unconscionable (and fruitless) to tell such parents, and the rest of society, that they must abandon condemnation of such crimes.

There have been widespread calls for the abolition of prison; *The Harvard Law Review* even published a special edition on the matter in 2019. Ben-Moshe (2020) says the idea is not as strange as it seems since the United States did something similar in the deinstitutionalization of psychiatric patients. What a success that was! It contributed to an epidemic of homelessness, the mentally ill being housed in prisons and jails, and "boarded" in emergency rooms around the country (Nordstom et al., 2019). The naivete of such views is astounding. We only have to look at what occurred in 2020 with calls for defunding the police and the decrease of proactive policing following the death of George Floyd in Minneapolis at the hands of the police. The FBI's Uniform Crime Report (2021) reported a 30% increase in homicides in 2020 over 2019, the largest single-year increase ever recorded, and the largest ever one-year decrease in arrests (24%). Moreover, the police cleared only 54% of the homicides in 2020, the lowest clearance rate ever recorded. The police used to clear up to 90% in the 1960s when most people respected them and cooperated with them (Keel, Jarvis, & Muirhead, 2009). By way of contrast, homicide clearance rates have remained steady in Western Europe for many years, ranging from an average of 98% in Finland to 80% in Sweden (Liem et al., 2019). This is what happens when the threat of arrest and punishment is significantly diminished.

By a large margin, most support for defunding the police was found among liberals (49%) (Edwards-Levy & Robillard, 2020). I assume that the greater tendency of liberals to hold an external locus of control and their free will skepticism leads them to view people's behavior as beyond their control, which probably accounts for their punishment abolitionist stance. We hold people morally responsible for what they do only if we believe that they have the ability to make reasoned choices to act or not to act morally. If we abandon such a belief, we invite the kind of anarchy and crime witnessed in 2020. As Mike Materni (2013, p. 288) opines:

> maybe Nietzsche was right when he quipped, "A little revenge is more human than no revenge." Moreover, given the fact that our retributivist instincts run so deep and may even play a part in our evolution, we may not—probably, even, should not—completely ban retribution from the realm of criminal punishment, if we want the criminal law and the criminal justice system to be respected and supported by the very society it was created to protect and serve.

However, if we engage a variety of emotions in the service of punishment, emotions also militate against disproportionate punishment. The human instinct for fairness generates opprobrium against unjust punishment, and benefits could be derived from strategies of reconciliation and reintegration with minor criminal offenders. A simple strategy of like-for-like reciprocity is highly effective for generating cooperative behavior in small groups, but game theorists have repeatedly shown that if two strict tit-for-tat strategists play and one cheats, it tends to launch a long series of tit-for-tat punitive responses that result in mutual loss. Game theorists find that a measure of forgiveness works better to maintain social cooperation rather than always paying back cheats in kind (Rand, Ohtsuki & Nowak, 2009). If people always punish noncooperation, they risk losing a valuable relationship if the cheating incident was uncharacteristic of a cheater who shows promise.

The forgiveness strategy responds to a one-shot betrayal with cooperation rather than retaliation in the next round of the game, and in most circumstances, it will return players to mutual cooperation. If it does not, victims will revert to punishment. Inviting cooperation in the face of defection is not a "sucker" strategy because it is not one that tolerates continued cheating. A forgiveness strategy is like sentencing first-time offenders to probation rather than prison, thus giving them an opportunity to redeem themselves and leaving the door open to future mutually advantageous cooperation between offenders and their communities. The probation sanction is still a response to criminal behavior, but the retaliation is conciliatory rather than punitive. Both offenders and their communities benefit from methods that express disapproval but that also conform to the reintegrative ideal. If we always respond to defectors with strong punishment, the community risks losing a potential future cooperator and offenders risk losing their connections to the community. This engages Caruso's (2021) public health model without the absurd notions of abandoning the concept of crime or abolishing prisons.

References

Agnew, R. (2013). Integrating assumptions about crime, people, and society: Response to the reviews of toward a unified criminology. *Journal of Theoretical & Philosophical Criminology, 5*, 74.

Al-Hoorie, A. (2014). Human agency: Does the beach ball have free will? In Z. Dörnyei, A. Henry, & P. MacIntyre (Eds.), *Motivational dynamics in language learning* (pp. 55–72). Bristol: Multilingual Matters.

Badcock, C. (2000). *Evolutionary psychology: A critical introduction*. Cambridge: Polity Press.

Bagaric, M., Hunter, D., & Svilar, J. (2021). Prison abolition: From naïve idealism to technological pragmatism. *The Journal of Criminal Law & Criminology, 111*, 351–406.

Baker, L., Bezdjian, S., & Raine, A. (2006). Behavior genetics: The science of antisocial behavior. *Law and Contemporary Problems, 69*, 7–46.

Barker, V. (2006). The politics of punishing: Building a state governance theory of American imprisonment variation. *Punishment & Society*, 8, 5–32.

Bartels, M., & Hudziak, J. (2007). Genetically informative designs in the study of resilience in developmental psychopathology. *Child and Adolescent Psychiatric Clinics of North America, 16*, 323–339.

Baumeister, R. (2008). Free will in scientific psychology. *Perspectives on Psychological Science, 3*, 14–19.

Baumeister, R. (2014). Constructing a scientific theory of free will. In W. Sinnott-Armstrong (Ed.), *Moral psychology, vol. 4. Free will and moral responsibility* (pp. 235–255). Cambridge, MA: MIT Press.

Baumeister, R., & Brewer, L. (2012). Believing versus disbelieving in free will: Correlates and consequences. *Social and Personality Psychology Compass, 6*, 736–745.

Beccaria, C. (1963). *On crimes and punishment* (H. Paulucci, Trans.). Indianapolis, IN: Bobbs–Merrill.

Ben-Moshe, L. (2020). *Decarcerating disability: Deinstitutionalization and prison abolition*. Minneapolis, MI: University of Minnesota Press.

Bentham, J. (1789 [1948]). *A fragment on government and an introduction to the principles of morals and legislation* (W. Harrison, Ed.). Oxford: Basil.

Bohr, N. (1950). On the notions of causality and complementarity. *Science, 111*, 51–54.

Bordone, M., Salman, M., Titus, H., Amini, E., Andersen, J., Chakraborti, B., … Braga de Freitas, G. (2019). The energetic brain–A review from students to students. *Journal of Neurochemistry, 151*, 139–165.

Bouchard, T., & McGue, M. (2003). Genetic and environmental influences on human psychological differences. *Journal of Neurobiology, 54*, 4–45.

Box, S. (1987). *Recession, crime and punishment*. Totowa, NJ: Barnes & Noble.

Brembs, B. (2011). Towards a scientific concept of free will as a biological trait: Spontaneous actions and decision-making in invertebrates. *Proceedings of the Royal Society: Biological Sciences, 278*, 930–939.

Brian, D. (1995). *The voice of genius: Conversations with Nobel scientists and other luminaries*. Cambridge, MA: Perseus Publishing.

Brunero, J. (2002). Evolution, altruism and internal reward explanations. *Philosophical Forum, 33*, 413–424.

Buckholtz, J., & Marois, R. (2012). The roots of modern justice: Cognitive and neural foundations of social norms and their enforcement. *Nature Neuroscience, 13*, 655–661.

Buckley, A. (2017). Is consciousness just an illusion? *BBC News*. https://www.bbc.com/news/science-environment-39482345.

Burt, C., & Simons, R. (2014). Pulling back the curtain on heritability studies: Biosocial criminology in the postgenomic era. *Criminology*, *52*, 223–262.

Burt, S. (2009). Rethinking environmental contributions to child and adolescent psychopathology: A meta-analysis of shared environmental influences. *Psychological Bulletin*, *135*, 608–637.

Canton, R. (2015). Crime, punishment and the moral emotions: Righteous minds and their attitudes towards punishment. *Punishment & Society*, *17*, 54–72.

Carey, G. (2003). *Human genetics for the social sciences*. Thousand Oaks, CA: Sage.

Caruso, G. (2021). Précis of rejecting retributivism: Free will, punishment, and criminal justice. *Journal of Legal Philosophy*, *46*, 120–125.

Chalmers, D. (1995). Facing up to the problem of consciousness. *Journal of Consciousness Studies*, *2*, 200–219.

Chalmers, D. (1996). *The conscious mind: In search of a fundamental theory*. Oxford: Oxford University Press.

Chalmers, D. (2017). The hard problem of consciousness. In S. Schneider & M. Velmans (Eds.), *The Blackwell companion to consciousness* (pp. 225–235). Malden, MA: Blackwell.

Crescioni, A., Baumeister, R., Ainsworth, S., Ent, M., & Lambert, N. (2016). Subjective correlates and consequences of belief in free will. *Philosophical Psychology*, *29*, 1–23.

Csikszentmihalyi, M., & Wong, M. (2014). The situational and personal correlates of happiness: A cross-national comparison. In M. Csikszentmihalyi (Ed.), *Flow and the foundations of positive psychology* (pp. 193–212). Dordrecht: Springer.

Ciaramidaro, A., Toppi, J., Casper, C., Freitag, C. M., Siniatchkin, M., & Astolfi, L. (2018). Multiple-brain connectivity during third party punishment: An EEG hyperscanning study. *Scientific Reports*, *8*, 1–13.

Clark, T. (2007). *Encountering naturalism: A worldview and its uses*. Somerville, MA: The Center for Naturalism.

Clarke, R., & Cornish, D. (2001). Rational choice. In R. Paternoster & R. Bachman (Eds.), *Explaining criminals and crime: Essays in contemporary criminological theory* (pp. 23–42). Los Angeles, CA: Roxbury.

Clarkson, J., Chambers, J., Hirt, E., Otto, A., Kardes, F., & Leone, C. (2015). The self-control consequences of political ideology. *Proceedings of the National Academy of Sciences of the United States of America*, *112*, 8250–8253.

Cohen, L., & Felson, M. (1979). Social change and crime rate trends: A routine activities approach. *American Sociological Review*, *44*, 588–608.

Cooper, J., Walsh, A., & Ellis, L. (2010). Is criminology ripe for a paradigm shift? Evidence from a survey of American criminologists. *Journal of Criminal Justice Education*, *21*, 332–347.

Cornish, D. & Clarke, R. (1987). Understanding crime displacement: An application of rational choice theory. *Criminology*, 25, 933-948.

Cosby, B., & Poussaint, A. (2007). *Come on, people: On the path from victims to victors*. Nashville, TN: Thomas Nelson.

Crick, F. (1994). *The astonishing hypothesis: The scientific search for the soul*. New York: Charles Scribner's Sons.

Curren, D., & Renzetti, C. (2001). *Theories of crime*. Boston, MA: Allyn & Bacon.

Currie, E. (1989). Confronting crime: Looking toward the twenty-first century. *Justice Quarterly*, *6*, 5–25.

Dahiru, H., & Oshishepo, S. (2019). Influence of locus of control and family background on criminal behaviour. *African Journal of Social and Behavioural Sciences*, *9*, 122–132.

Descartes, R., de Spinoza, B., & Hutchins, R. (1952). *Great books of the western world*. Chicago, IL: Encyclopaedia Britannica.

De Quervain, D., Fischbacher, U., Valerie, T., Schellhammer, M., Schnyder, U., Buch, A., & Fehr, E. (2004). The neural basis of altruistic punishment. *Science*, *305*, 1254–1259.

de Waal, F. (1996). *Good natured: The origins of right and wrong in humans and other animals*. Cambridge, MA: Harvard University Press.

Dias, M., Partington, M., Section on Neurologic Surgery, Ragheb, J., Aldana, P., Gruber, D., Jea, A., Bauer, R., Brockmeyer, D., & Ritter, A. (2015). Congenital brain and spinal cord malformations and their associated cutaneous markers. *Pediatrics*, *136*, e1105–e1119.

Dilman, I. (2013). *Free will: An historical and philosophical introduction*. New York: Routledge.

dos Santos, M., Rankin, D., & Wedekind, C. (2011). The evolution of punishment through reputation. *Proceedings of the Royal Society: Biology*, *278*, 371–377.

Durant, W. (1944). *Caesar and Christ*. New York: Simon and Schuster.

Durkheim, E. (1997). *The division of labor in society*. New York: The Free Press.

Ekins, E. (2019). Poll: What Americans think cause wealth and poverty. Cato Institute. https://www.cato.org/blog/poll-what-americans-think-cause-wealth-poverty.

Edwards-Levy, A., & Robillard, K. (2020). Most Americans want police reform but don't back 'defund the police'. *Huffington Post*, June 15.

Einstein, A., & Infeld, L. (1938). *The evolution of physics*. Cambridge: Cambridge University Press.

Eliaeson, S. (2002). *Max Weber's methodologies: Interpretation and critique*. Malden, MA: Blackwell Press.

Farnier, J., Shankland, R., Kotsou, I., Inigo, M., Rosset, E., & Leys, C. (2021). Empowering well-being: Validation of a locus of control scale specific to well-being. *Journal of Happiness Studies*, *22*, 3513–3542.

Federal Bureau of Investigation. (2021). *Crime in the United States: 2020*. Washington, DC: U.S. Government Printing Office.

Feldman, G. (2017). Making sense of agency: Belief in free will as a unique and important construct. *Social and Personality Psychology Compass*, *11*, 1–15.

Ferri, E. (1917). *Criminal sociology*. Boston, MA: Little, Brown.

Fincher, J. (1982). *The human brain: Mystery of matter and mind*. Washington, DC: U.S. News Books.

Frankenberry, N. (2008). *The faith of scientists: In their own words*. Princeton, NJ: Princeton University Press.

Fromm, E. (1956). *The art of loving*. New York: Bantam.

Georgiev, D. (2020). Quantum information theoretic approach to the mind–brain problem. *Progress in Biophysics and Molecular Biology*, *158*, 16–32.

Gierowski, J., & Rajtar, T. (2003). Chosen factors influencing the locus of control in perpetrators of criminal acts. *Problems of Forensic Sciences*, *103*, 129–138.

Gottesman, I., & Hanson, D. (2005). Human development: Biological and genetic processes. *Annual Review of Psychology*, *56*, 263–286.

Gottfredson, M. (2011). Sanctions, situations, and agency in control theories of crime. *European Journal of Criminology*, *8*, 128–143.

Gottfredson, M., & Hirschi, T. (1990). *A general theory of crime*. Stanford, CA: Stanford University Press.

Gould, S. (1997). Foreword: The positive power of skepticism. In M. Shermer (Ed.), *Why people believe weird things* (pp. i-iv). New York: W.H. Freeman.

Greene, J., & Cohen, J. (2004). For the law, neuroscience changes nothing and everything. *Philosophical Transactions of the Royal Society of London. Series B: Biological Sciences*, *359*, 1775–1785.

Haidt, J. (2001). The emotional dog and its rational tail: A social intuitionalist approach to moral judgment. *Psychological Review*, *108*, 814–834.

Hannikainen, I., Cabral, G., Machery, E., & Struchiner, N. (2017). A deterministic worldview promotes approval of state paternalism. *Journal of Experimental Social Psychology*, *70*, 251–259.

Hatch, V. L., & Walsh, A. (2016). *Capital punishment: Theory and practice of the ultimate penalty*. New York: Oxford University Press.

Hatemi, P., McDermott, R., & Eaves, L. (2015). Genetic and environmental contributions to relationships and divorce attitudes. *Personality and Individual Differences*, *72*, 135–140.

Hawking, S., & Mlodinow, L. (2010). *The grand design*. New York: Bantam Books.

Hawthorne, N. (2003). *The scarlet letter*. New York: Barnes & Nobel Classics.

Hecht, E. (2007). Energy and change. *The Physics Teacher*, *45*, 88–92.

Heffernan, R., & Ward, T. (2017). A comprehensive theory of dynamic risk and protective factors. *Aggression and Violent Behavior*, *37*, 129–141.

Henrich, J., McElreath, R., Barr, A., Ensminger, J., Barrett, C., Bolyanatz, A., Cardenas, J. C., … Ziker, J. (2006). Costly punishment across human societies. *Science, 312*, 1767–1770.

Hills, T. (2019). Neurocognitive free will. *Proceedings of the Royal Society B, 286*(1908), 20190510.

Hirschi, T. (2017). On the compatibility of rational choice and social control theories of crime. In D. Cornish & R. Clarke (Eds.), *The reasoning criminal* (pp. 105–118). New York: Routledge.

Hirschi, T., & Hindelang, M. (1977). Intelligence and delinquency: A revisionist review. *American Sociology Review, 42*, 571–587.

Holt, J. (2012). *Why does the world exist? An existential detective story.* New York: WW Norton & Company.

Huby, P. (1967). The first discovery of the free will problem. *Philosophy, 42*, 353–362.

Jamieson, A., & Radick, G. (2017). Genetic determinism in the genetics curriculum. *Science & Education, 26*, 1261–1290.

Jones, O., & Shen, F. (2012). Law and neuroscience in the United States. In T. Spranger (Ed.), *International neurolaw: A comparative analysis* (pp. 349–380). Berlin: Springer-Verlag.

Kant, I. (1964). *Groundwork of the metaphysics of morals* (H. Paton, Trans.). New York: Harper & Row.

Kauffman, S., & Radin, D. (2021). Is brain-mind quantum? A theory and supporting evidence. arXiv preprint arXiv:2101.01538.

Keel, T., Jarvis, J., & Muirhead, Y. (2009). An exploratory analysis of factors affecting homicide investigations: Examining the dynamics of murder clearance rates. *Homicide Studies, 13*, 50–68.

Klein, R. (2012). The neurobiology of altruistic punishment: A moral assessment of its social utility. In K. Plaisance & T. Reydon (Eds.), *Philosophy of behavioral biology* (pp. 297–313). Boston, MA: Springer Science.

Krstić, M. (2022). Rational choice theory–alternatives and criticisms. *Socijalna ekologija: časopis za ekološku misao i sociologijska istraživanja okoline, 31*, 9–27.

Kruk, E. (2012). Arguments for an equal parental responsibility presumption in contested child custody. *The American Journal of Family Therapy, 40*, 33–55.

Levy, N., & Bayne, T. (2004). A will of one's own: Consciousness, control, and character. *International Journal of Law and Psychiatry, 27*(5).

Li, C., Wang, S., Zhao, Y., Kong, F., & Li, J. (2017). The freedom to pursue happiness: Belief in free will predicts life satisfaction and positive affect among Chinese adolescents. *Frontiers in Psychology, 7*, Article 2027.

Libet, B. (1985). Unconscious cerebral initiative and the role of conscious will in voluntary action. *Behavioral and Brain Sciences, 8*, 529–539.

Libet, B. (1999). Do we have free will? *Journal of Consciousness Studies, 6*, 47–57.

Libet, B., Wright Jr, E., & Gleason, C. (1983). Preparation-or intention-to-act, in relation to pre-event potentials recorded at the vertex. *Electroencephalography and Clinical Neurophysiology, 56*, 367–372.

Liem, M., Suonpää, K., Lehti, M., Kivivuori, J., Granath, S., Walser, S., & Killias, M. (2019). Homicide clearance in Western Europe. *European Journal of Criminology, 16*, 81–101.

Lilly, J., Cullen, F., & Ball, R. (2011). *Criminological Theory: Context and Consequences* (5th ed.). Thousand Oaks, CA: Sage.

Logan, C., & Gaes, G. (1993). Meta-analysis and the rehabilitation of punishment. *Justice Quarterly, 10*, 245–263.

Lombroso, C. (1876). *Criminal man*. Milan: Hoepli.

Lombroso-Ferrero, G. (1972). *Criminal man according to the classification of Cesare Lombroso.* Montclaire, NJ: Patterson Smith.

Massey, D. (2002). A brief history of human society: The origin and role of emotion in social life. *American Sociological Review, 67*, 1–29.

Marteni, M. (2013). Criminal punishment and the pursuit of justice. *British Journal of American Legal Studies, 2*, 263–304.

Mazzarello, P. (2011). Cesare Lombroso: An anthropologist between evolution and degeneration. *Functional Neurology, 26*, 97–101.

Mayford, M., Siegelbaum, S., & Kandel, E. (2012). Synapses and memory storage. *Cold Spring Harbor Perspectives in Biology, 4*, 1–19.

McBride, K. (2007). *Punishment and the political order.* Ann Arbor, MI: University of Michigan Press.

McGilchrist, I. (2009). *The master and his emissary: The divided brain and the making of the western world.* New Haven, CT: Yale University Press.

Menninger, K. (1968). *The crime of punishment.* New York: Penguin Books.

Miller, W. (1958). Lower–class culture as a generating milieu of gang delinquency. *Journal of Social Issues, 14,* 5–19.

Miller, J., & Lynham, D. (2001). Structural models of personality and their relation to antisocial behavior: A meta-analytic review. *Criminology, 39,* 765–798.

Millikan, R. (1927). *Evolution in science and religion.* New Haven, CT: Yale University Press.

Mitchell, K. (2007). The genetics of brain wiring: From molecule to mind. *PLoS Biology, 4,* 690–692.

Moffitt, T., & Beckley, A. (2015). Abandon twin research? Embrace epigenetic research? Premature advice for criminologists. *Criminology, 53,* 121–126.

Moll, J., Krueger, F., Zahn, R., Pardini, M., de Oliveira-Souza, R., & Grafman, J. (2006). Human fronto-mesolimbic networks guide decisions about charitable donation. *Proceedings of the National Academy of Sciences of the United States of America, 103,* 15623–15628.

Morse, M. (2006). Brain overclaim syndrome and criminal responsibility: A diagnostic note. *Ohio State Journal of Criminal Law, 3,* 397–412.

Muthukrishna, M., Doebeli, M., Chudek, M., & Henrich, J. (2018). The cultural brain hypothesis: How culture drives brain expansion, sociality, and life history. *PLoS Computational Biology, 14*(11), e1006504.

Nes, R., & Røysamb, E. (2017). Happiness in behaviour genetics: An update on heritability and changeability. *Journal of Happiness Studies, 18,* 1533–1552.

Nes, R., Røysamb, E., Tambs, K., Harris, J., & Reichborn-Kjennerud, T. (2006). Subjective well-being: Genetic and environmental contributions to stability and change. *Psychological Medicine, 36,* 1033–1042.

Nestor, P. (2019). In defense of free will: Neuroscience and criminal responsibility. *International Journal of Law and Psychiatry, 65,* 101344.

Nettler, G. (1984). *Explaining crime* (3rd ed.). New York: McGraw Hill.

Nielsen, F. (2006). Achievement and ascription in educational attainment: Genetic and environmental influences on adolescent schooling. *Social Forces, 85,* 193–216.

Nordstrom, K., Berlin, J., Nash, S., Shah, S., Schmelzer, N., & Worley, L. (2019). Boarding of mentally ill patients in emergency departments: American Psychiatric Association resource document. *Western Journal of Emergency Medicine, 20,* 690–695.

Nye, R. (1976). Heredity or milieu: The foundations of modern European criminological theory. *Isis, 67,* 335–355.

Ouyang, M., Dubois, J., Yu, Q., Mukherjee, P., & Huang, H. (2019). Delineation of early brain development from fetuses to infants with diffusion MRI and beyond. *Neuroimage, 185,* 836–850.

Paulhus, D., & Carey, J. (2011). The FAD–Plus: Measuring lay beliefs regarding free will and related constructs. *Journal of Personality Assessment, 93,* 96–104.

Penney, S. (2012). Impulse control and criminal responsibility. *International Journal of Law and Psychiatry, 35,* 99–103.

Pereboom, D. (2008). A compatibilist account of the epistemic conditions on rational deliberation. *The Journal of Ethics, 12,* 287–306.

Planck, M. (2017). *Where is science going?* New York: W.W. Norton.

Plato. (1960). *The republic and other works.* Garden City, NY: Doubleday.

Pleasants, N. (2019). Free will, determinism and the "problem" of structure and agency in the social sciences. *Philosophy of the Social Sciences, 49,* 3–30.

Pockett, S. (2007). The concept of free will: Philosophy, neuroscience and the law. *Behavioral Sciences & the Law, 25,* 281–293.

Polderman, T., Benyamin, B., De Leeuw, C., Sullivan, P., Van Bochoven, A., Visscher, P., & Posthuma, D. (2015). Meta-analysis of the heritability of human traits based on fifty years of twin studies. *Nature Genetics, 47,* 702–709.

Rachels, J. (1986). *The elements of moral philosophy.* New York: Random House.

Rand, D., Ohtsuki, H., & Nowak, M. (2009). Direct reciprocity with costly punishment: Generous tit-for-tat prevails. *Journal of Theoretical Biology, 256*, 45–57.

Reznik, R. (2019). Retributive abolitionism. *Berkeley Journal of Criminal Law, 24*, 123–194.

Ridley, M. (2003). *Nature via nurture: Genes, experience and what makes us human.* New York: Harper Collins.

Rigoni, D., Kühn, S., Gaudino, G., Sartori, G., & Brass, M. (2012). Reducing self-control by weakening belief in free will. *Consciousness and Cognition, 21*, 1482–1490.

Rose, S. (2001). Moving on from old dichotomies: Beyond nature-nurture towards a lifeline perspective. *British Journal of Psychiatry, 178*, 3–7.

Rosebury, B. (2009). Private revenge and its relation to punishment. *Utilatus, 21*, 1–21.

Roskies, A. (2006). Neuroscientific challenges to free will and responsibility. *Trends in Cognitive Sciences, 10*, 419–423.

Sampson, R. (2012). *Great American city: Chicago and the enduring neighborhood effect*. Chicago, IL: University of Chicago Press.

Schafer, S. (1976). The problem of free will in criminology. *The Journal of Criminal Law and Criminology, 67*, 481–485.

Schuster, P. (2009). Free will, information, quantum mechanics, and biology it pays to distinguish different forms of free choice and information. *Complexity, 15*, 8–11.

Schwekendiek, D. (2009). Height and weight differences between North and South Korea. *Journal of Biosocial Science, 41*, 51–55.

Seligman, M. (2002). *Authentic happiness*. New York: Free Press.

Selita, F., & Kovas, Y. (2019). Genes and Gini: What inequality means for heritability. *Journal of Biosocial Science, 51*, 18–47.

Sesardic, N. (2003). Heritability and indirect causation. *Philosophy of Science, 70*, 1002–1014.

Sharma, A., Blank, A., Patel, P., & Stein, K. (2013). Health care policy and regulatory implications on medical device innovations: A cardiac rhythm medical device industry perspective. *Journal of Interventional Cardiac Electrophysiology, 36*, 107–117.

Sharp, B. (2006). *Changing criminal thinking: A treatment program*. Alexandria, VA: American Correctional Association.

Singh, D., & Rani, A. (2017). A study of psychological (personality) correlates of criminal behaviour. *Indian Journal of Health and Wellbeing, 8*, 62–66.

Stillman, T., Baumeister, R., & Mele, A. (2011). Free will in everyday life: Autobiographical accounts of free and unfree actions. *Philosophical Psychology, 24*, 381–394.

Stillman, T., Baumeister, R., Vohs, K., Lambert, N., Fincham, F., & Brewer, L. (2010). Personal philosophy and personnel achievement: Belief in free will predicts better job performance. *Social Psychological and Personality Science, 1*, 43–50.

Stohr, M., & Walsh, A. (2019). *Corrections: The essentials*. Thousand Oaks, CA: Sage.

Sweetser, K. (2014). Partisan personality: The psychological differences between democrats and republicans, and independents somewhere in between. *American Behavioral Scientist, 58*, 1183–1194.

TenHouten, W. (2021). Hatred, life without love, and the descent into hell. In C. Mayer & E. Vanderheiden (Eds.), *International handbook of love* (pp. 699–717). Cham, Switzerland: Springer.

Tielbeek, J., Barnes, J., Popma, A., Polderman, T., Lee, J., Perry, J., … Boutwell, B. (2018). Exploring the genetic correlations of antisocial behaviour and life history traits. *British Journal of Psychology, 4*, 467–470.

Tooley, U., Bassett, D., & Mackey, A. (2021). Environmental influences on the pace of brain development. *Nature Reviews Neuroscience, 22*, 372–384.

Trudge, C. (1999). Who's afraid of genetic determinism? *Biologist, 46*, 96.

Tsai, J., Wang, C., & Lo, H. (2014). Locus of control, moral disengagement in sport, and rule transgression of athletes. *Social Behavior and Personality, 42*, 59–68.

Turkheimer, E. (2000). Three laws of behavior genetics and what they mean. *Current Directions in Psychological Science, 9*, 160–164.

Turkheimer, E. (2011). Genetics and human agency: Comment on Dar-Nimrod and Heine 2011. *Psychological Bulletin, 137*, 825–828.

Turkheimer, E., Haley, A., Waldron, M., D'Onofrio, B., & Gottesman, I. (2003). Socioeconomic status modifies heritability of IQ in young children. *Psychological Science*, *14*, 623–628.

Tuvblad, C., & Baker, L. (2011). Human aggression across the lifespan: Genetic propensities and environmental moderators. *Advances in Genetics*, *75*, 171–214.

Tuvblad, C., Grann, M., & Lichtenstein, P. (2006). Heritability for adolescent antisocial behavior differs with socioeconomic status: Gene–environment interaction. *Journal of Child Psychology and Psychiatry*, *47*, 734–743.

Twenge, J., Zhang, L., & Im, C. (2004). It's beyond my control: A cross-temporal meta-analysis of increasing externality in locus of control, 1960–2002. *Personality and Social Psychology Review*, *8*, 308–319.

Tyler, N., Heffernan, R., & Fortune, C. (2020). Reorienting locus of control in individuals who have offended through strengths-based interventions: Personal agency and the good lives model. *Frontiers in Psychology*, *11*, 553240.

Ule, A., Schram, A., Rieddl, A., & Cason, T. (2009). Indirect punishment and generosity toward strangers. *Science*, *326*, 1701–1704.

van den Haag, E. (2003). Justice, deterrence and the death penalty. In J. Aker, R. Bohm, & C. Lanier (Eds.), *America's experiment with capital punishment* (pp. 233–249). Durham, NC: Carolina Academic Press.

van Drunen, L., Dobbelaar, S., van der Cruijsen, R., van der Meulen, M., Achterberg, M., Wierenga, L., & Crone, E. (2021). The nature of the self: Neural analyses and heritability estimates of self-evaluations in middle childhood. *Human Brain Mapping*, *42*, 5609–5625.

van Inwagen, P. (1983). *An essay on free will*. Oxford: Oxford University Press.

Vohs, K., & Schooler, J. (2008). The value of believing in free will: Encouraging a belief in determinism increases cheating. *Psychological Science*, *19*, 49–54.

Vold, G., Bernard, T., & Snipes, J. (1998). *Theoretical criminology*. New York: Oxford University Press.

Wallace, W. (1990). Rationality, human nature, and society in Weber's theory. *Theory and Society*, *19*, 199–223.

Walsh, A. (1981). *Human nature and love: Biological, intrapsychic, and socio-behavioral perspectives*. Lanham, MD: University Press of America.

Walsh, A. (2022). Political ideology and happiness. *Mankind Quarterly*, *62*, 660–686.

Walsh, A., & Ellis, L. (2007). *Criminology: An interdisciplinary approach*. Thousand Oaks, CA: Sage.

Walsh, A., Johnson, H., & Bolen, J. (2012). Drugs, crime, and the epigenetics of hedonic allostasis. *Journal of Contemporary Criminal Justice*, *28*, 314–328.

Walsh, A., & Jorgensen, C. (2020). *Criminology: The essentials*. Thousand Oaks, CA: Sage.

Walsh, A., & Stohr, M. (2010). *Correctional assessment, casework, and counseling* (5th ed.). Alexandria, VA: American Correctional Association.

Walters, G. D. (2022). *Criminality and crime: A social-cognitive-developmental theory of delinquent and criminal behavior*. New York: Rowman & Littlefield.

Ward, D., Stafford, M., & Gray, L. (2006). Rational choice, deterrence, and theoretical integration. *Journal of Applied Social Psychology*, *36*, 571–585.

Weiss, A., Bates, T., & Luciano, M. (2008). Happiness is a personal (ity) thing: The genetics of personality and well-being in a representative sample. *Psychological Science*, *19*, 205–210.

Wiebe, R. (2011). The nature and utility of low self-control. In K. Beaver & A. Walsh (Eds.), *The Ashgate research companion to biosocial theories of crime* (pp. 369–395). Farnham: Ashgate.

White, A. (2004). *Substance use and the adolescent brain: An overview with the focus on alcohol*. Durham, NC: Duke University Medical Center.

Wigner, E. (1990). The unreasonable effectiveness of mathematics in the natural sciences. *Mathematics and Science*, *13*, 1–14.

Wigner, E. (2013). *The collected works of Eugene Paul Wigner: Historical, philosophical, and socio-political papers. Historical and biographical reflections and syntheses*. Berlin: Springer-Verlag.

Wilson, J. (1975). *Thinking about crime*. New York: Basic Books.

Wilson, J. (2000). *The marriage problem: How our culture has weakened families*. New York: HarperCollins.

Wilson, J., & Herrnstein, R. (1985). *Crime and human nature*. New York: Simon & Schuster.

Woollett, K., & Maguire, E. (2011). Acquiring “the knowledge” of London’s layout drives structural brain changes. *Current Biology*, *21*, 2109–2114.

Wright, R. (1995). Where there’s a will, there’s no way: The treatment of the choice debate in criminology textbooks, 1956 to 1965 and 1983 to 1992. *Teaching Sociology*, *23*, 8–15.

Wood, D. (2010). Punishment: Consequentialism. *Philosophy Compass*, *5*, 455–469.

Young, J. (2016). Voodoo criminology and the numbers game. In J. Ferrell, K. Hayward, W. Morrison, & M. Presdee (Eds.), *Cultural criminology unleashed* (pp. 27–42). London: Routledge-Cavendish.

Zimmerman, M. (2011). *The immorality of punishment*. Buffalo, NY: Broadview Press.

Index